A IS FOR ALPHA-SKETCH
ACTIVITY & COLORING BOOK
Vol. 1   by Bradd Parton

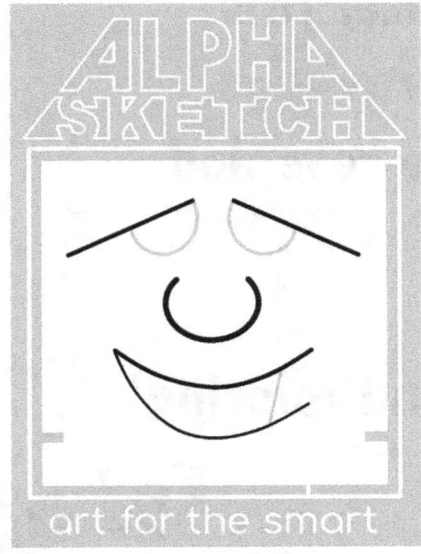

No portion of this book may be used or reproduced in any other manner whatsoever without the written permission of the author. The scanning, uploading, and distribution of this book via the Internet or any other means without the permission of the author is illegal and punishable by law. Permission is granted solely to the original purchaser to reproduce for classroom use. The Alpha-Sketch technique and the drawings herein including all related elements are trademarked and copyrighted by Bradd Parton. All rights reserved. The red background of the cover was designed by Freepik. A IS FOR ALPHA-SKETCH, VOL. 1 is copyright 2017. The illustrations in this book were created digitally.

For information regarding author visits or Alpha-Sketch fundraising opportunities contact braddparton@gmail.com. Visit us online at http://www.alpha-sketch.com.

What's an Alpha-Sketch?!

An Alpha-Sketch is a drawing made of only the 26 letters of the alphabet. Every line is a letter, and each letter is hidden once in the drawing. There are no omissions, repetitions, or extra lines.

See the bicycle on the cover? The front tire is the letter "G," for example. Can you find the rest?

Some letters could be considered interchangeable (ex. M is W upside down), but each letter is used only once. This collection features 40 of my drawings. All of the letters' locations are revealed in the back of the book.

Have fun finding the letters and coloring!

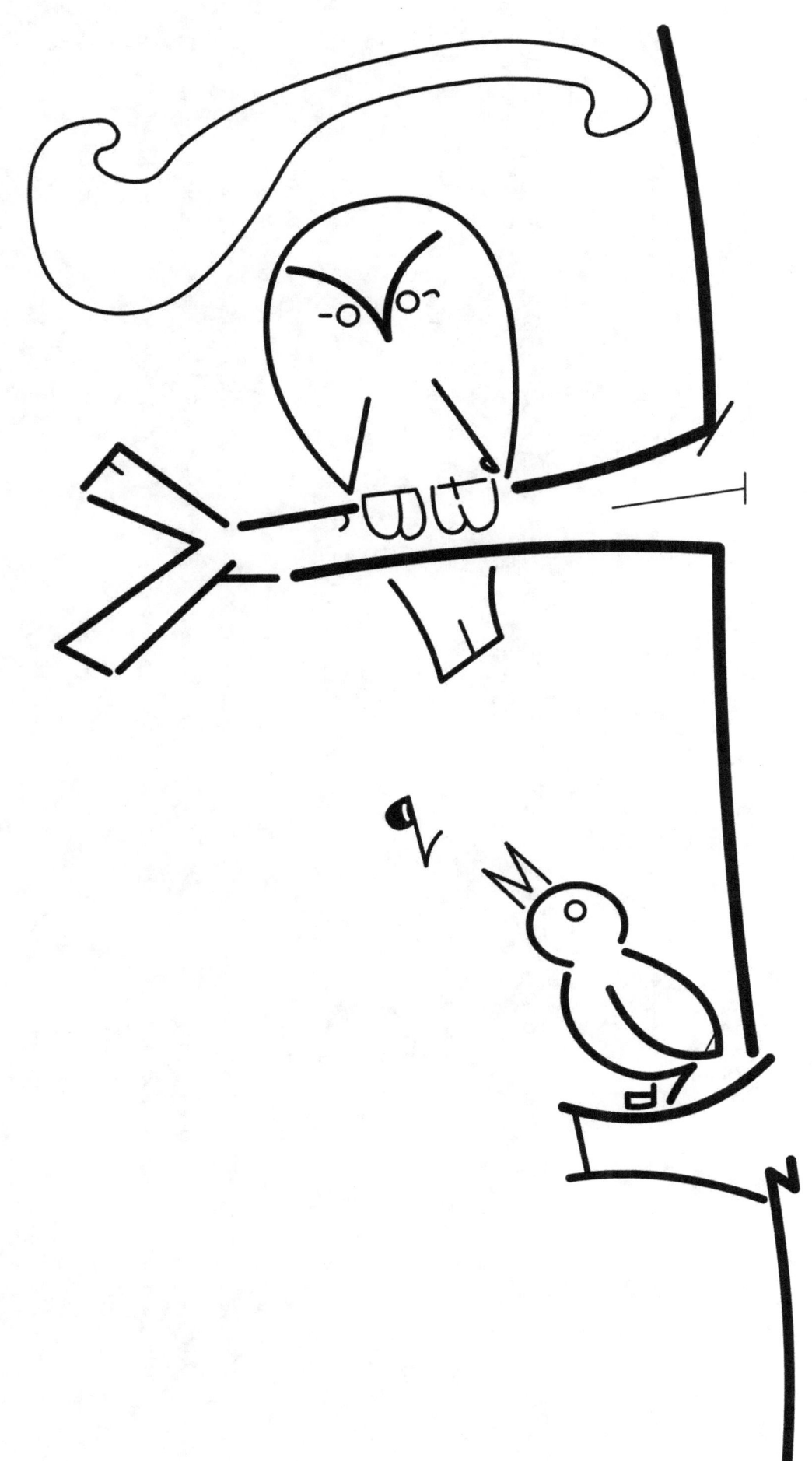

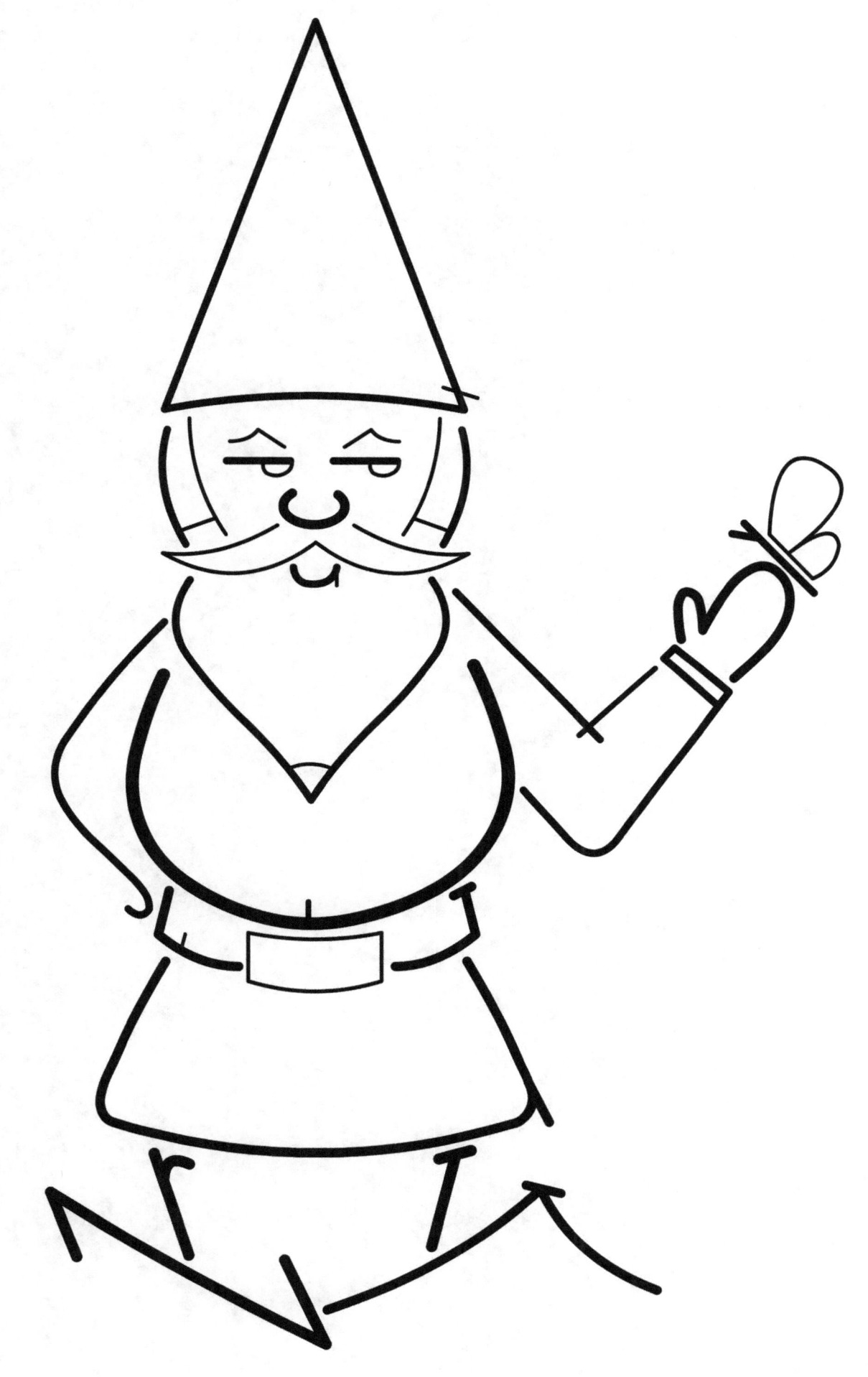

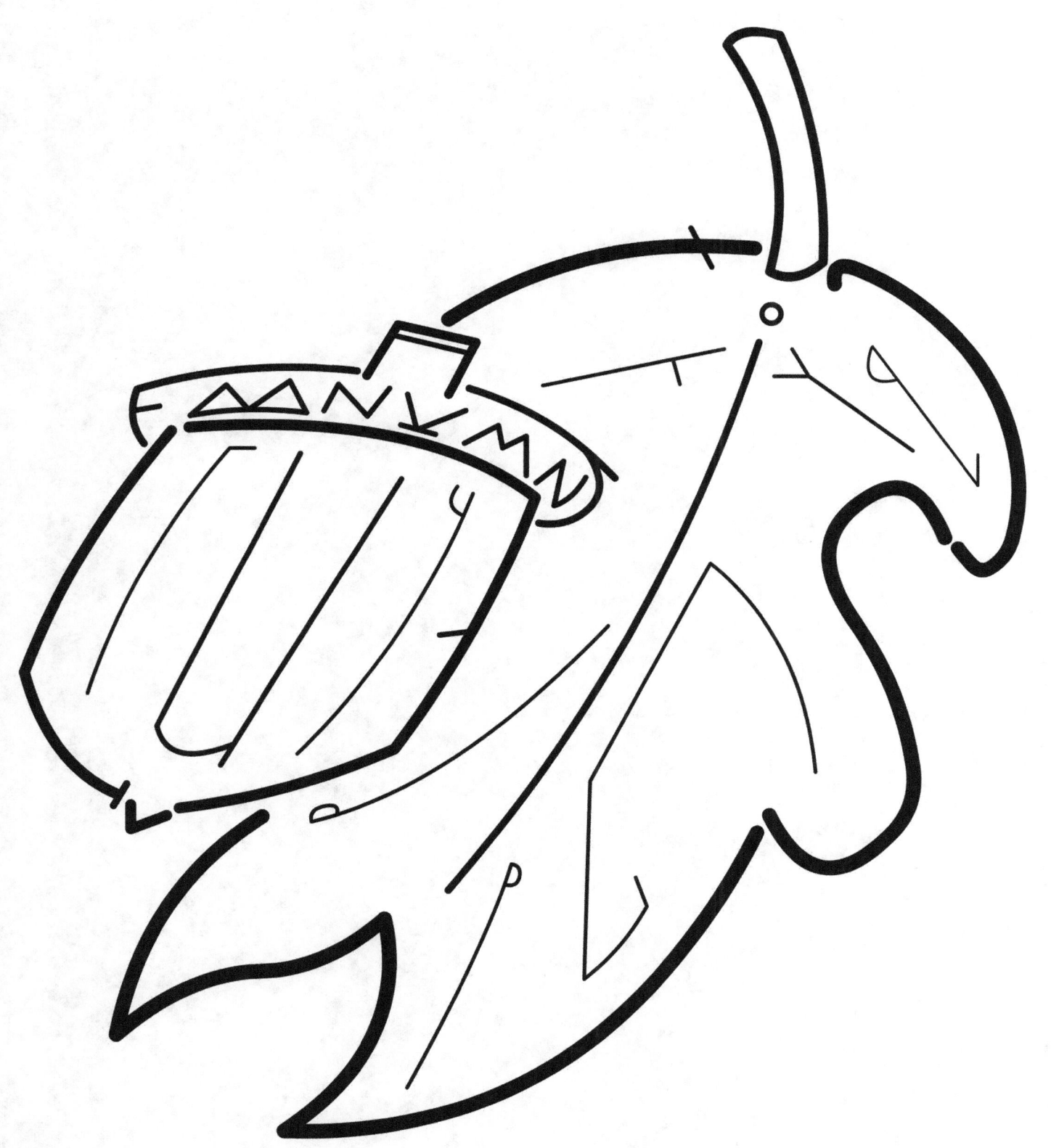

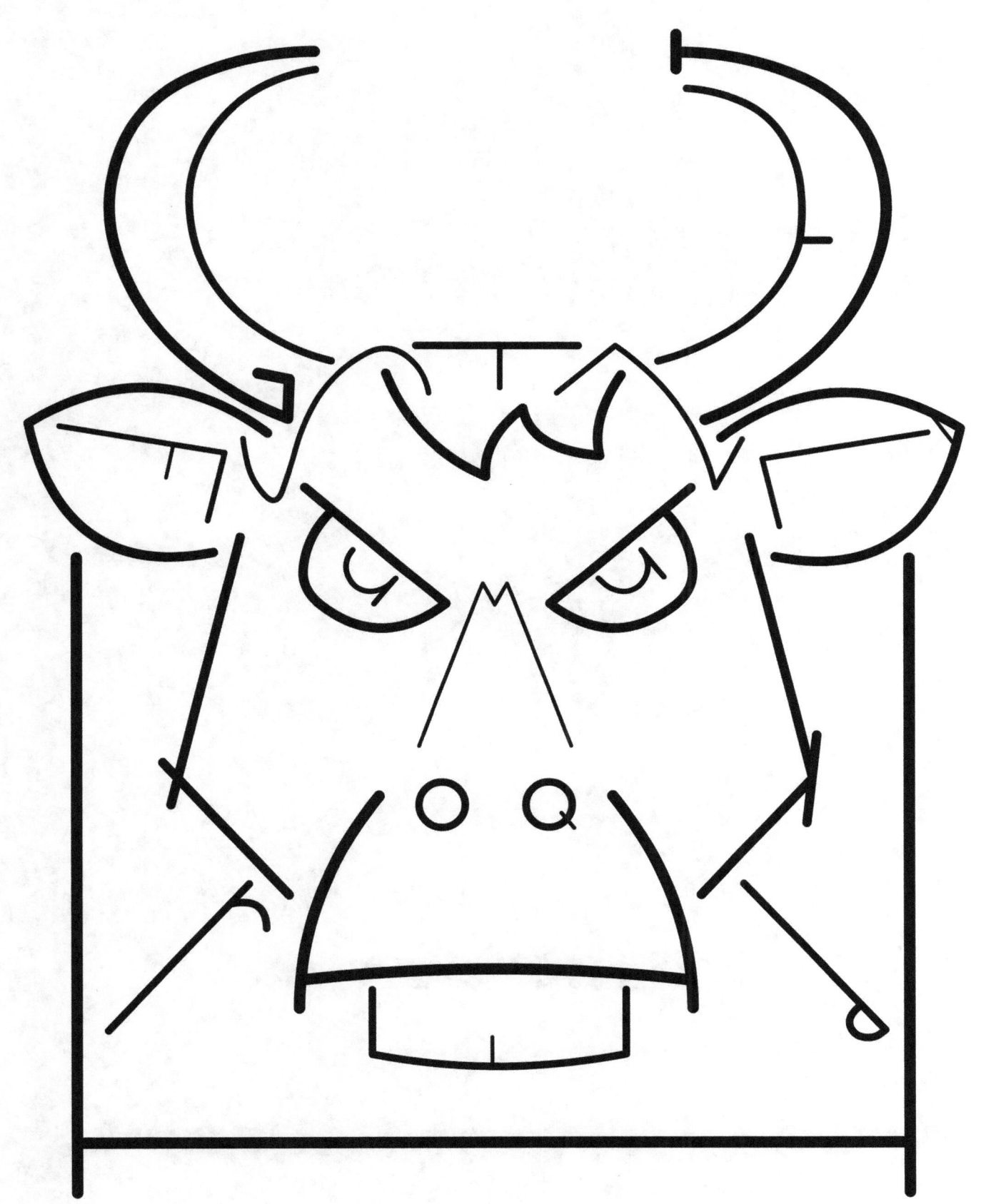

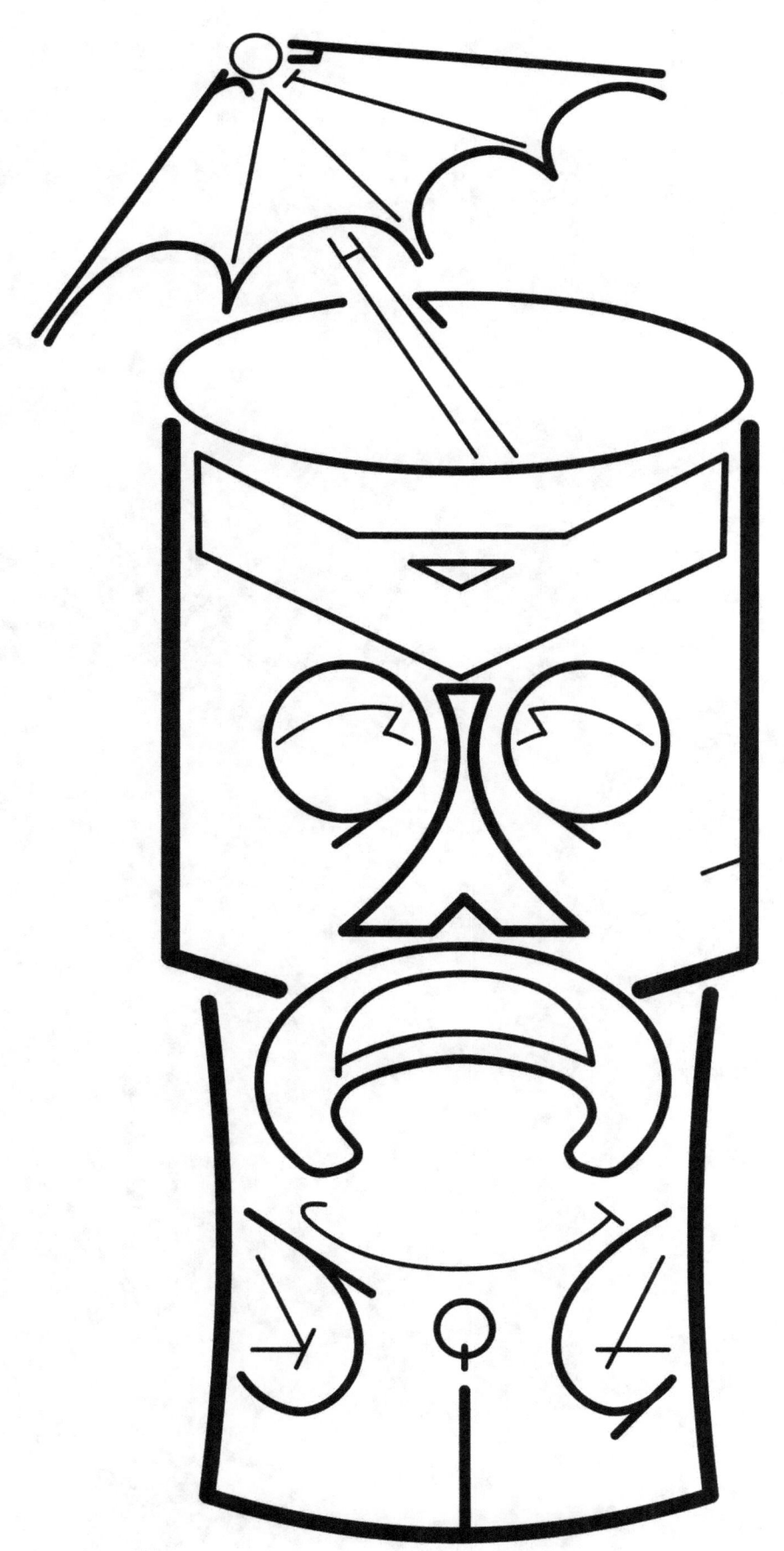

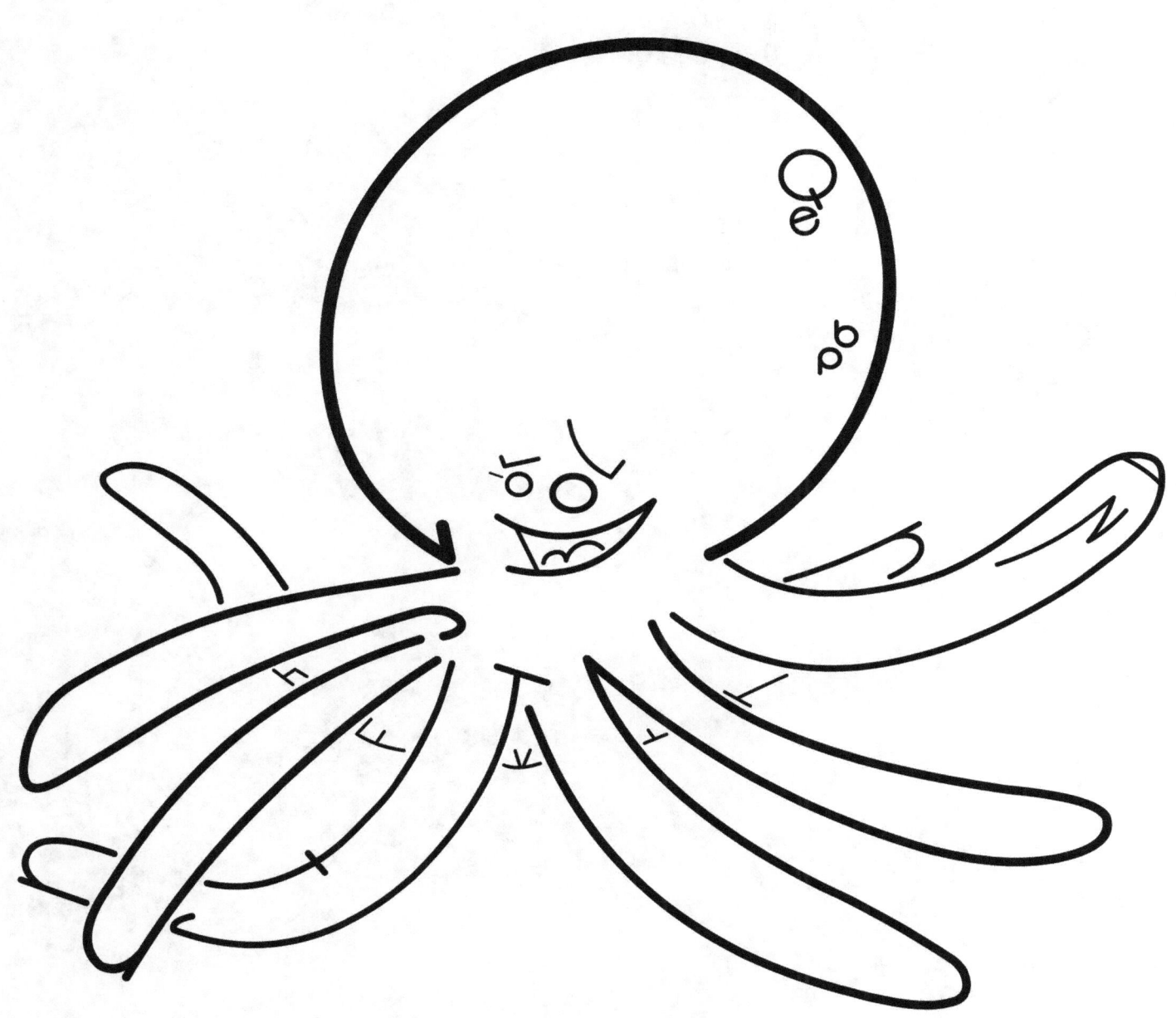

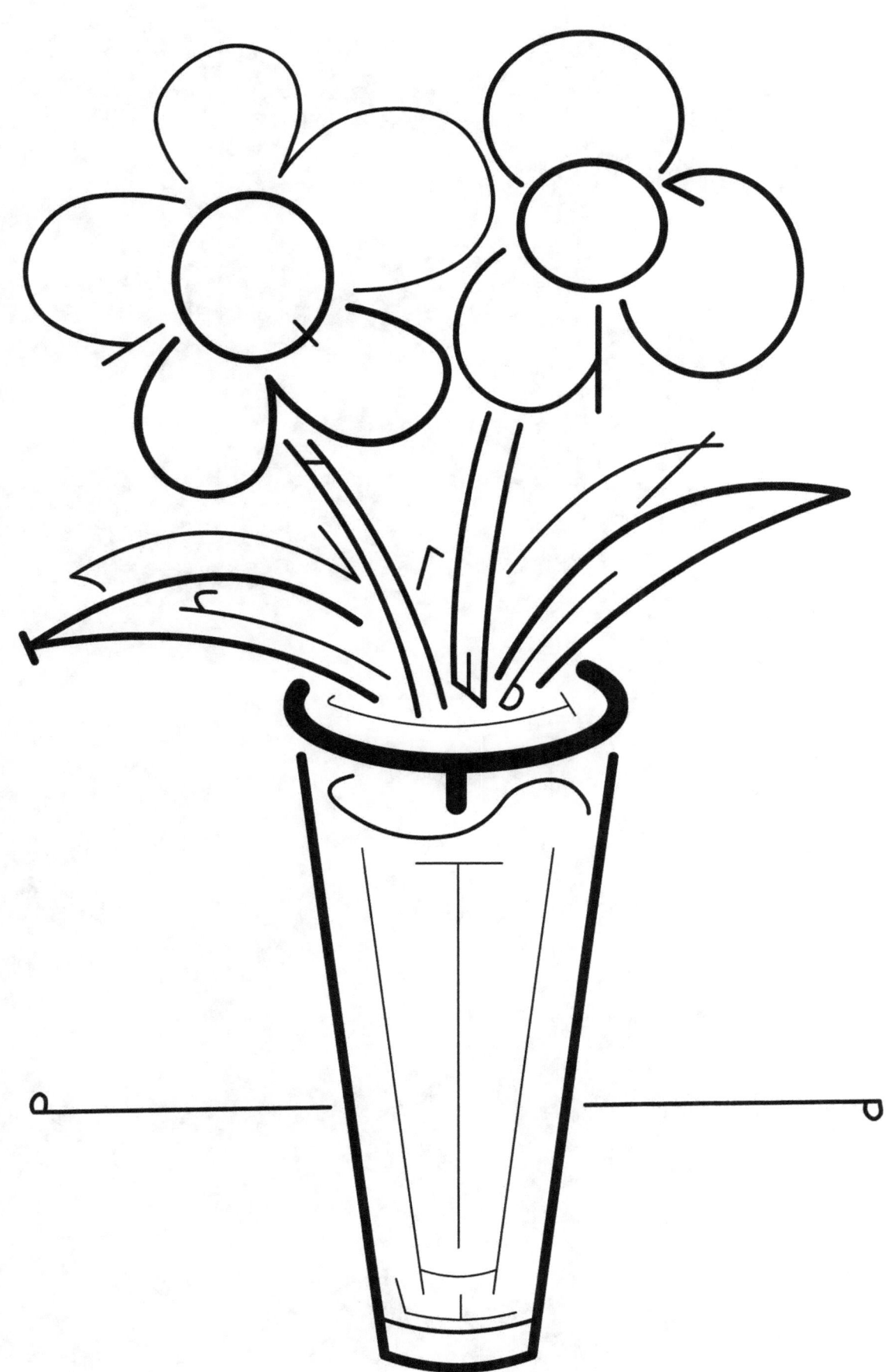

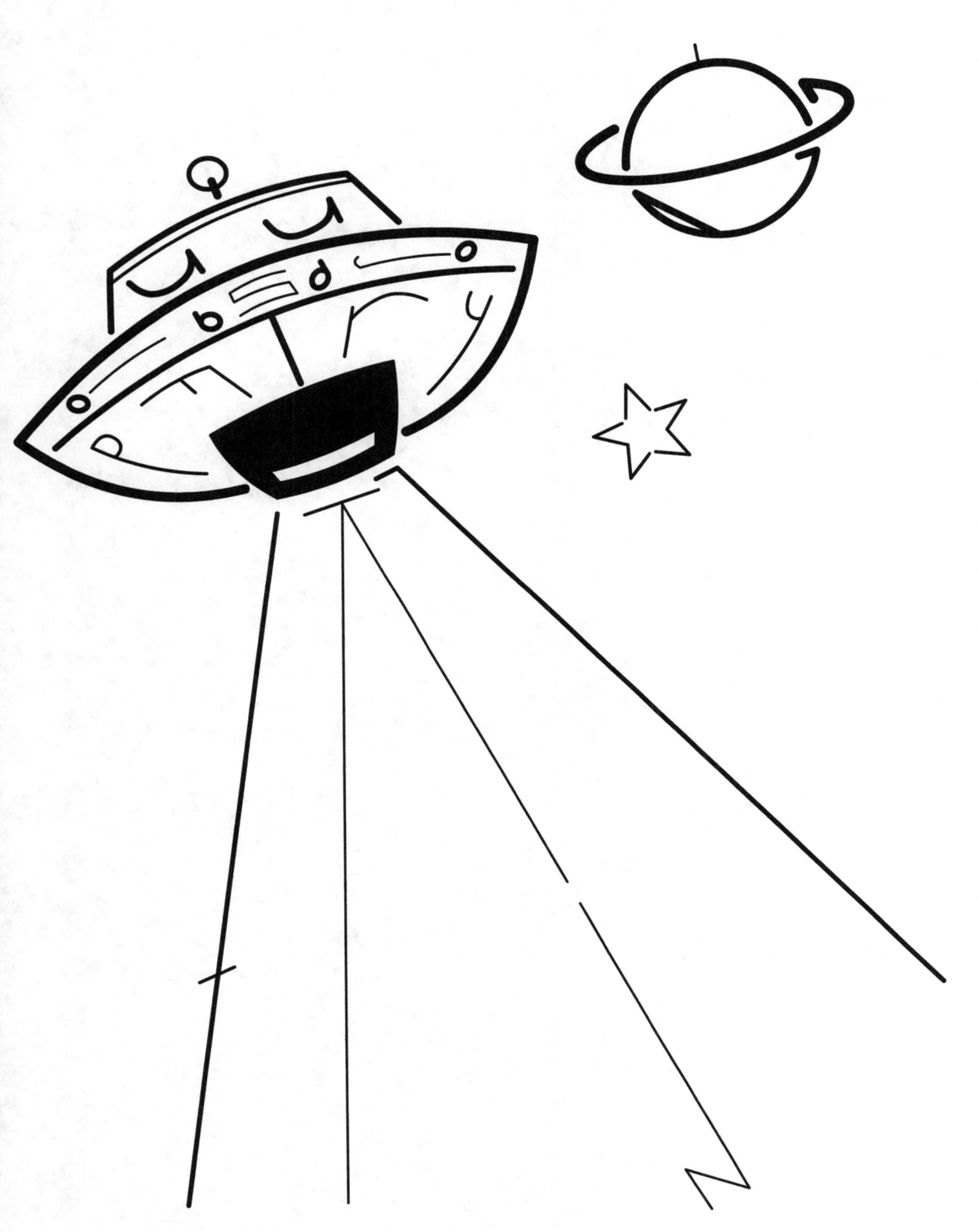

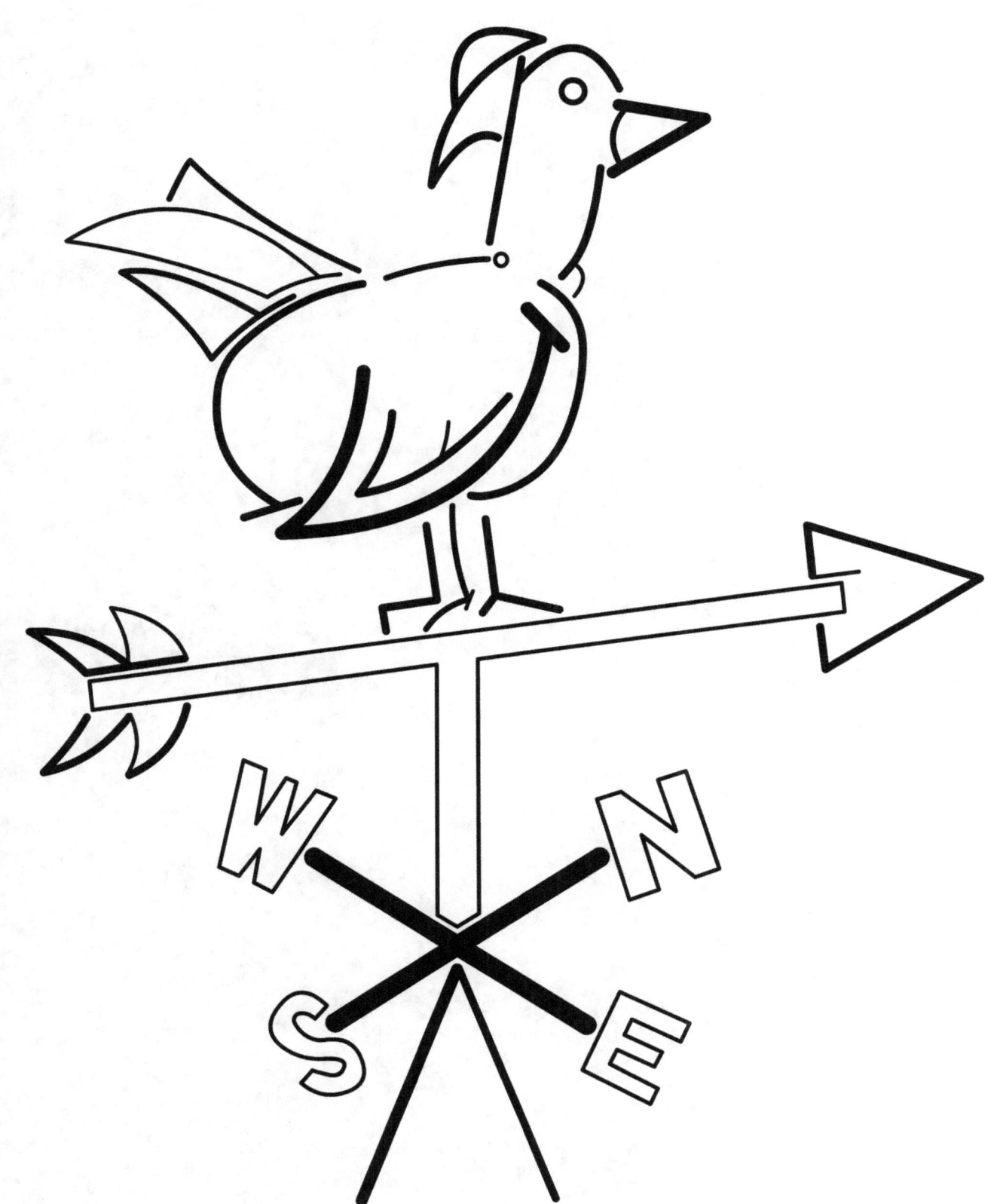

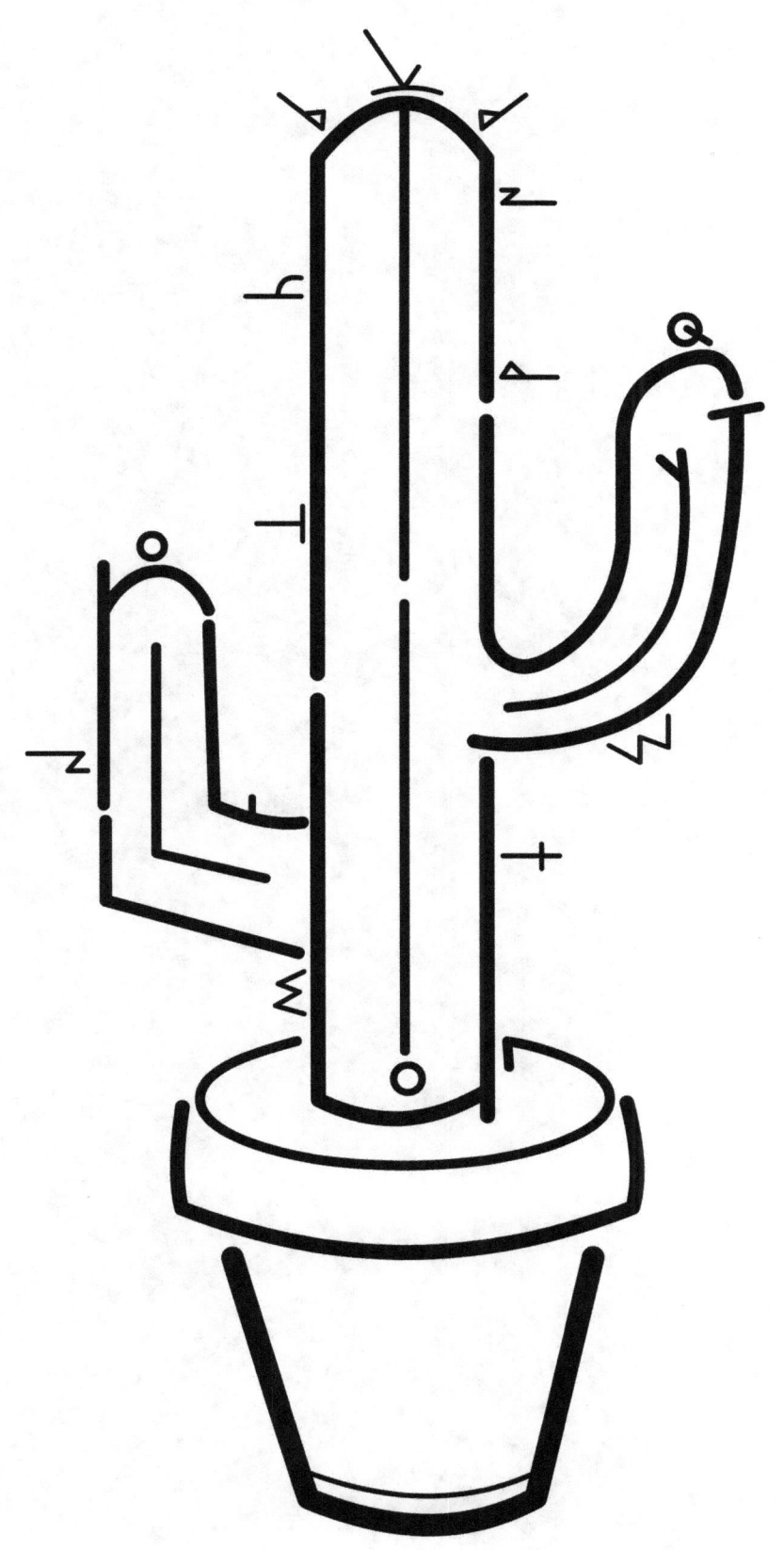

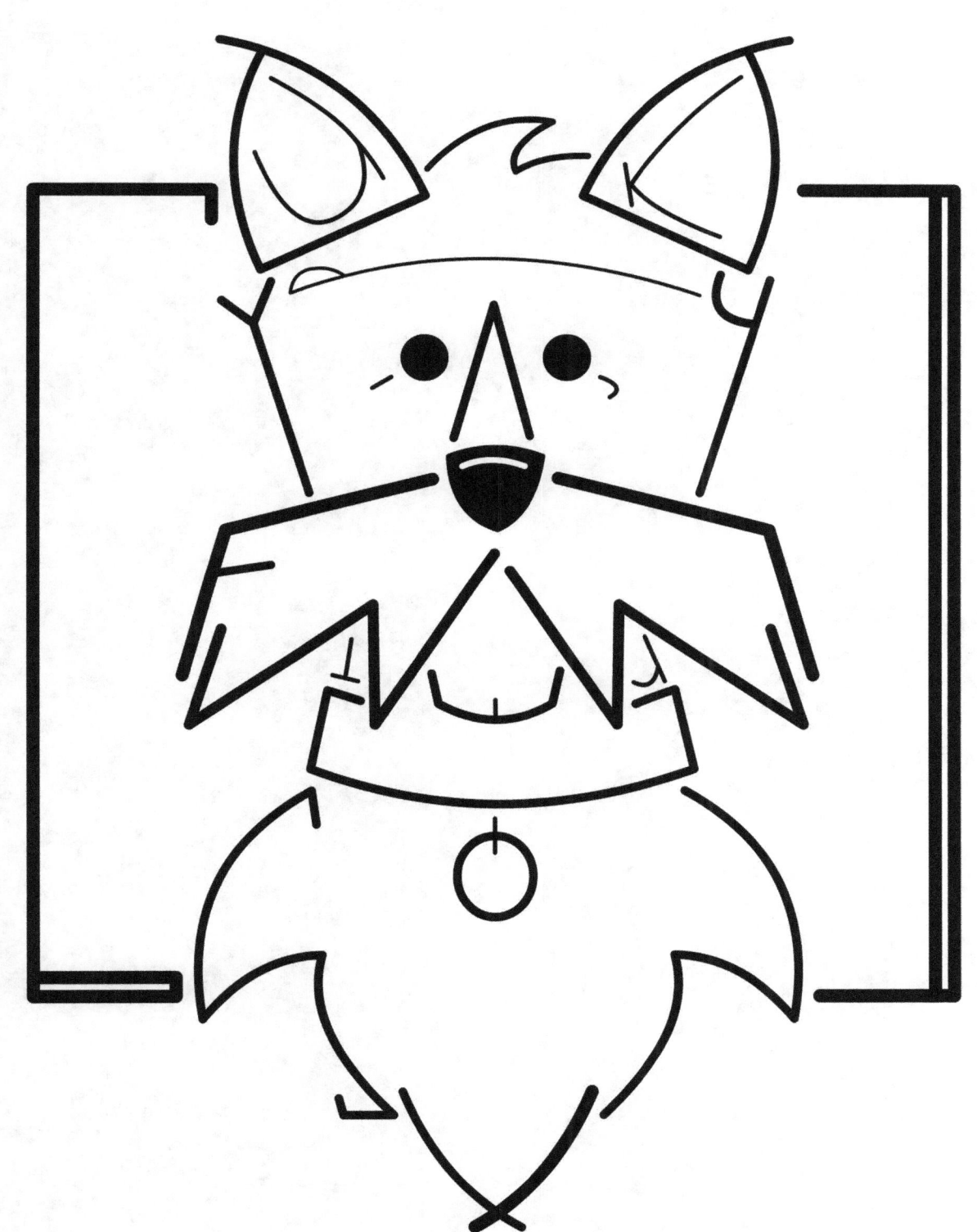

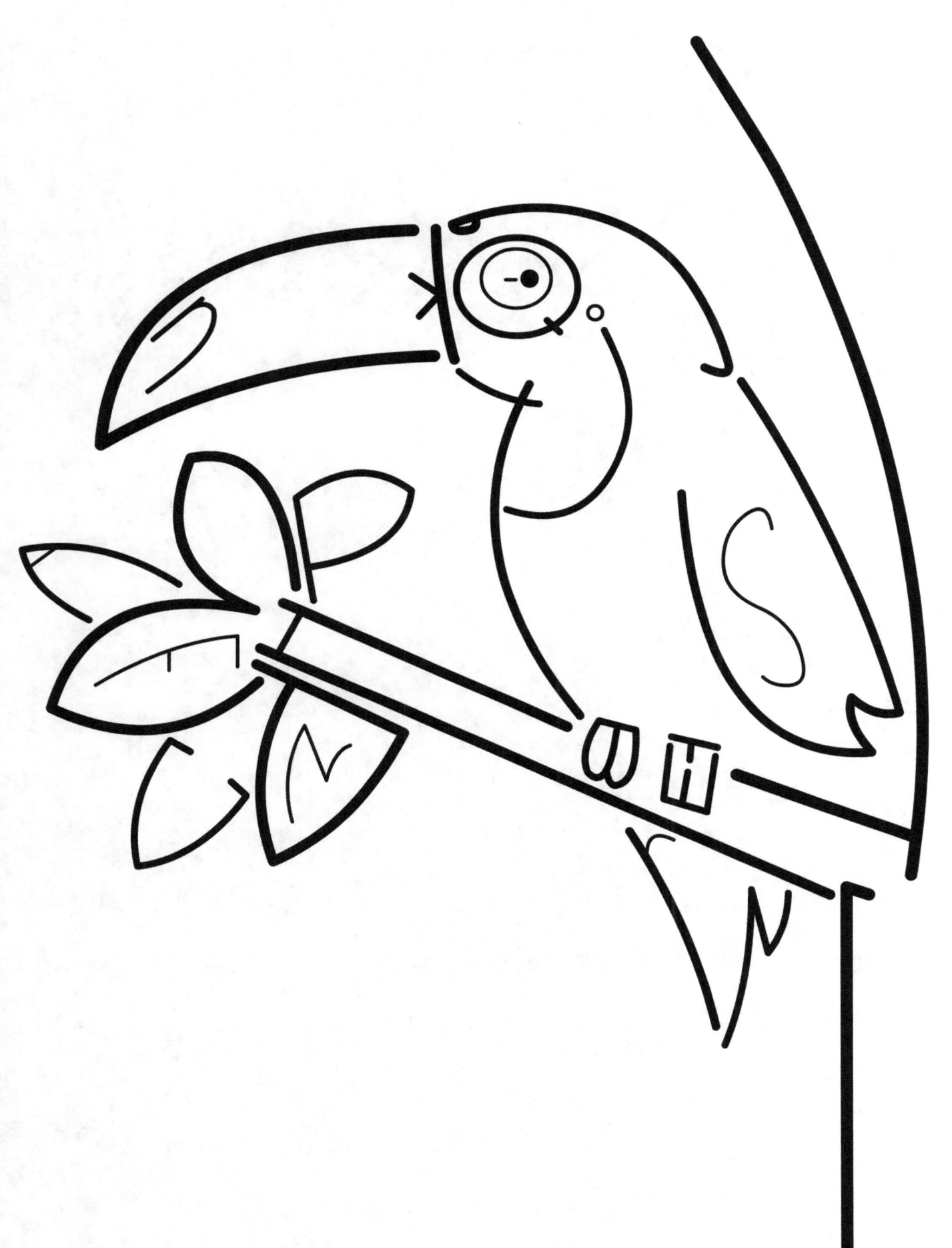

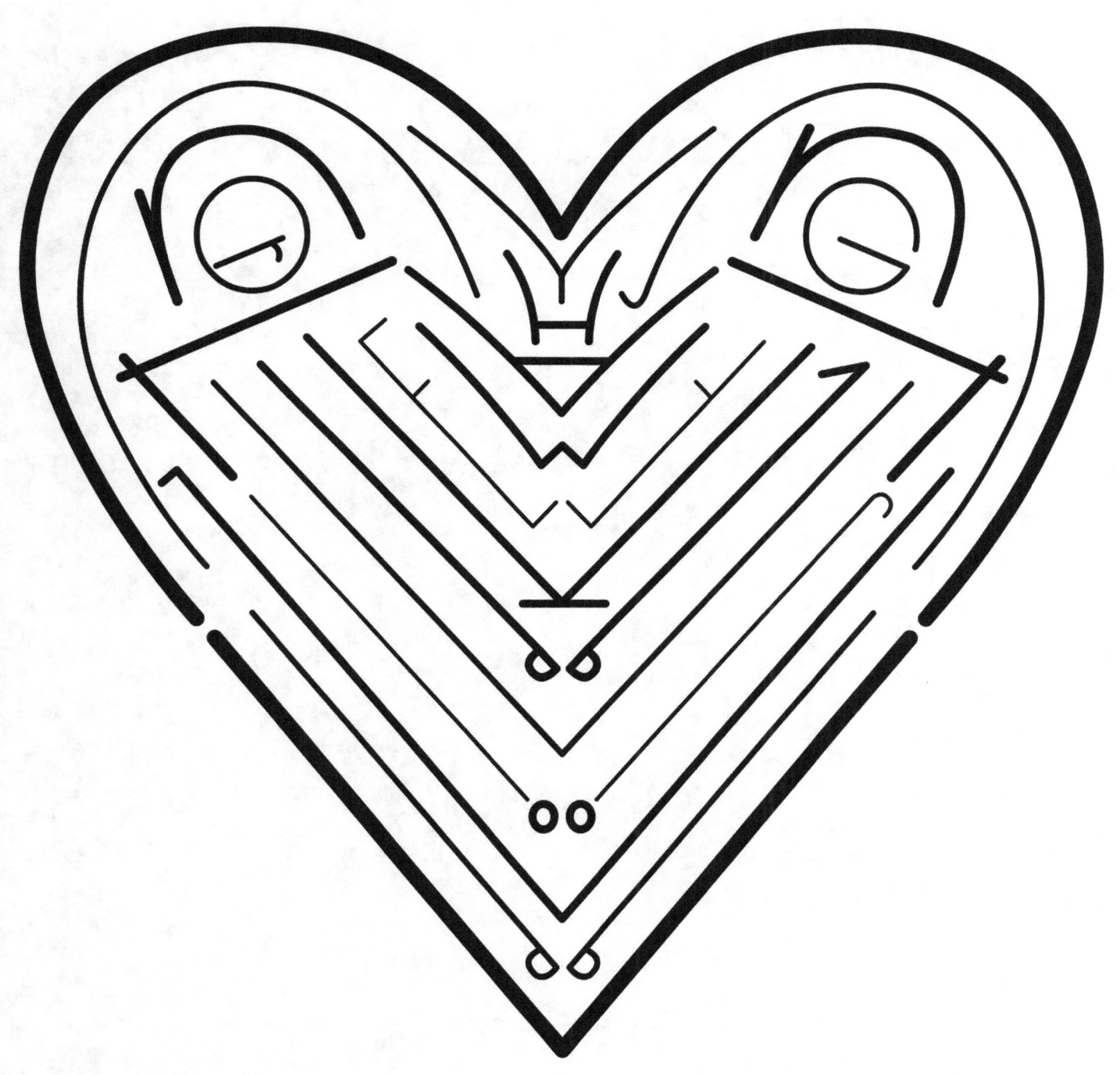

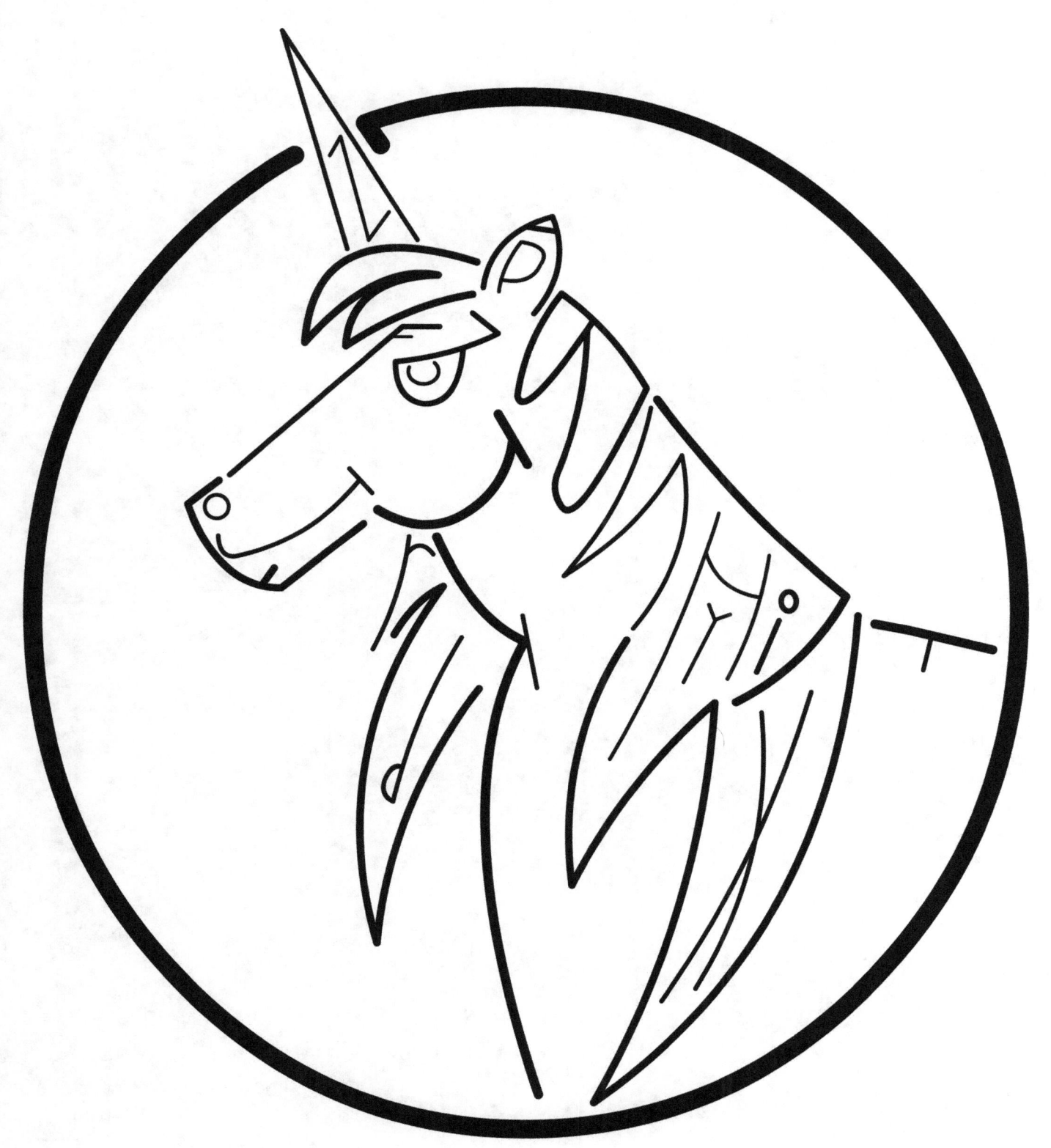

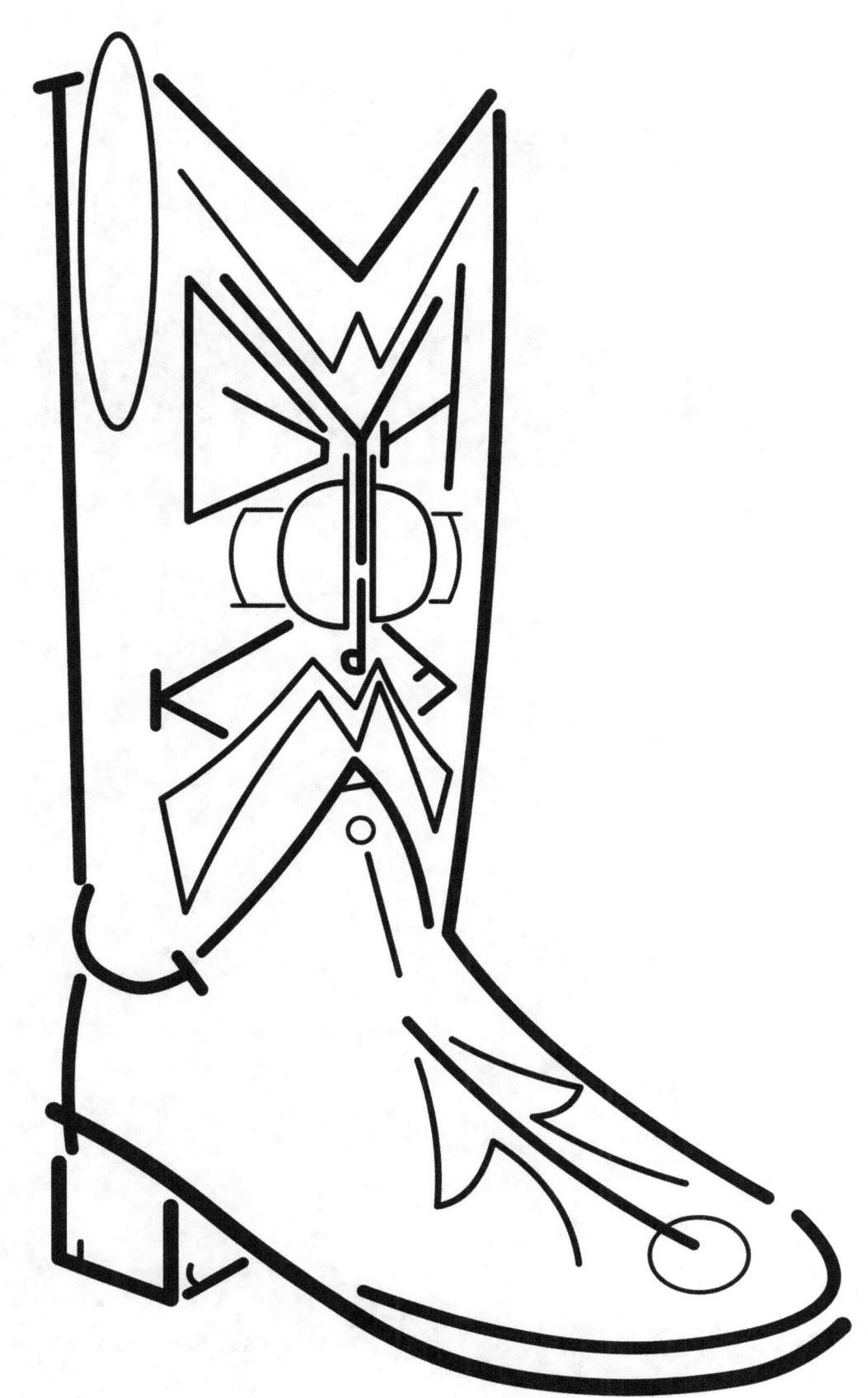

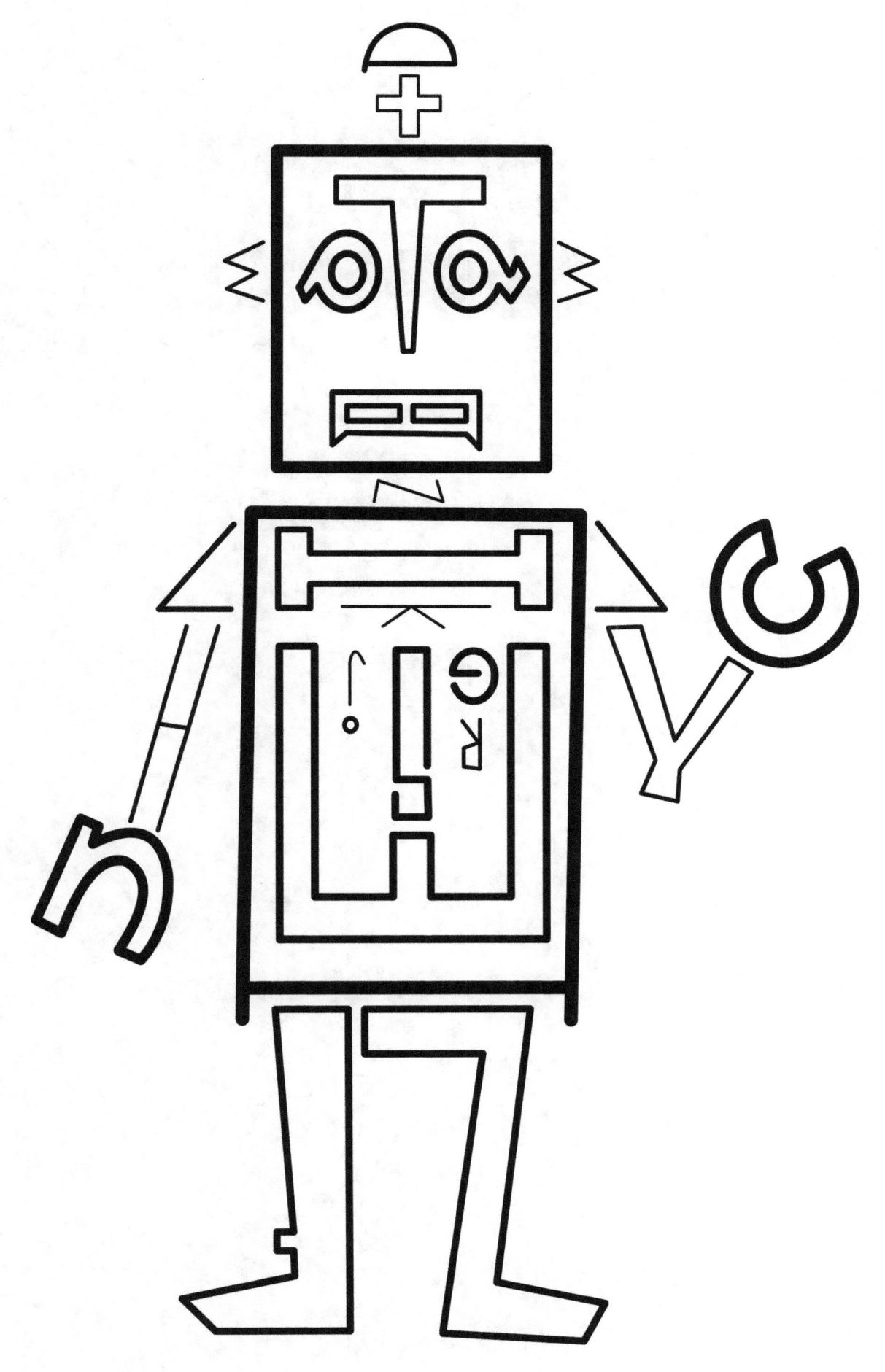

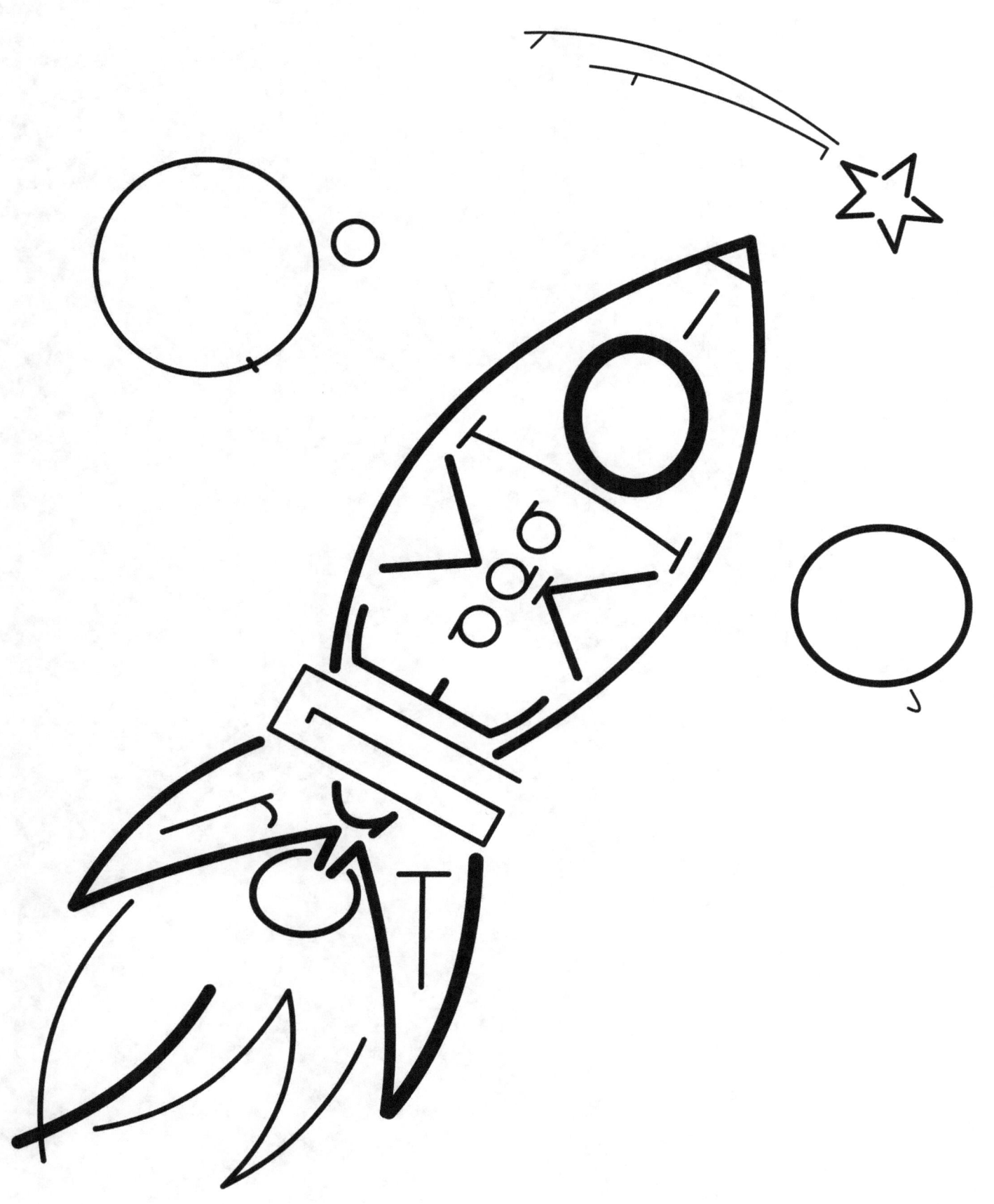

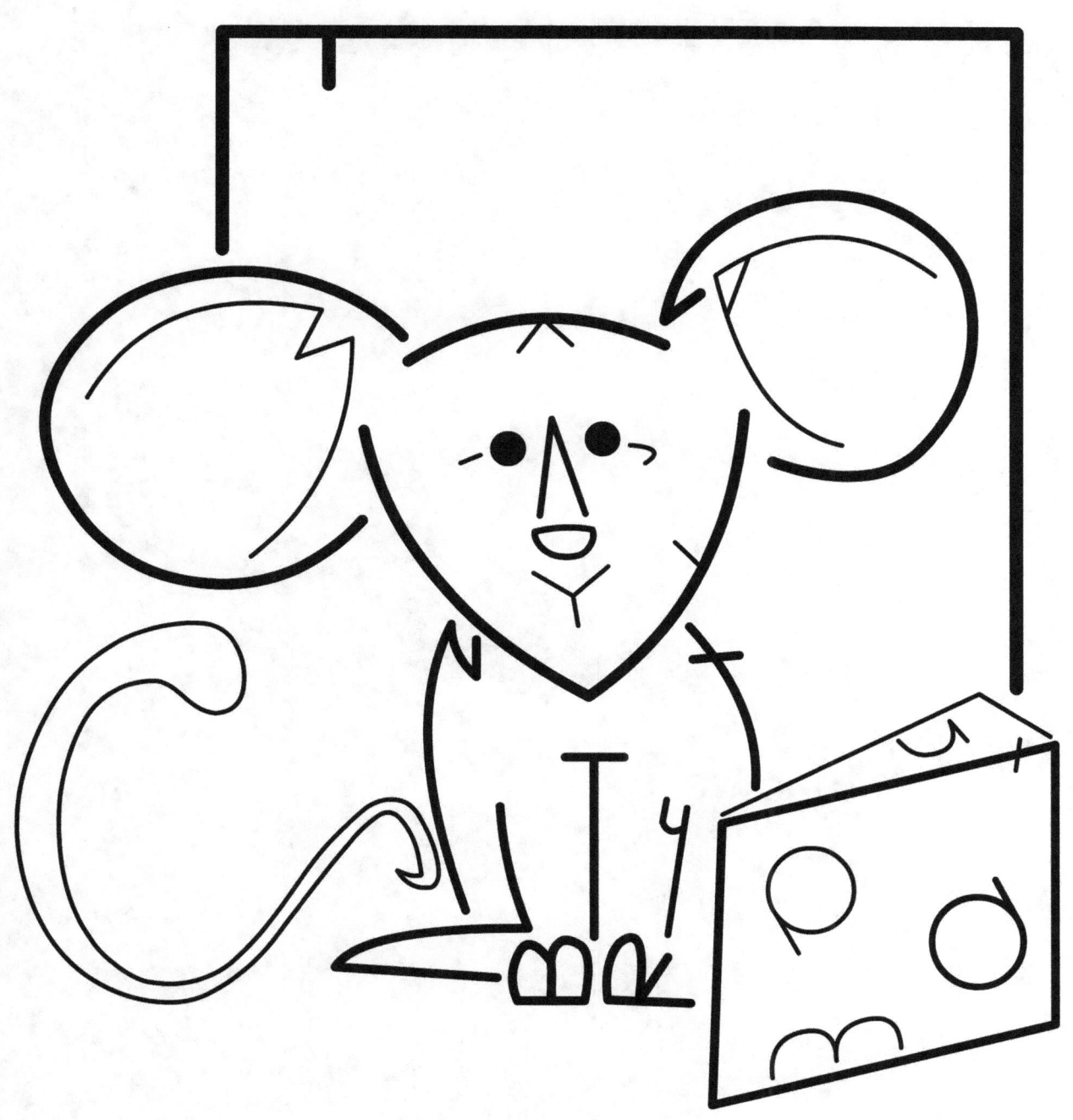

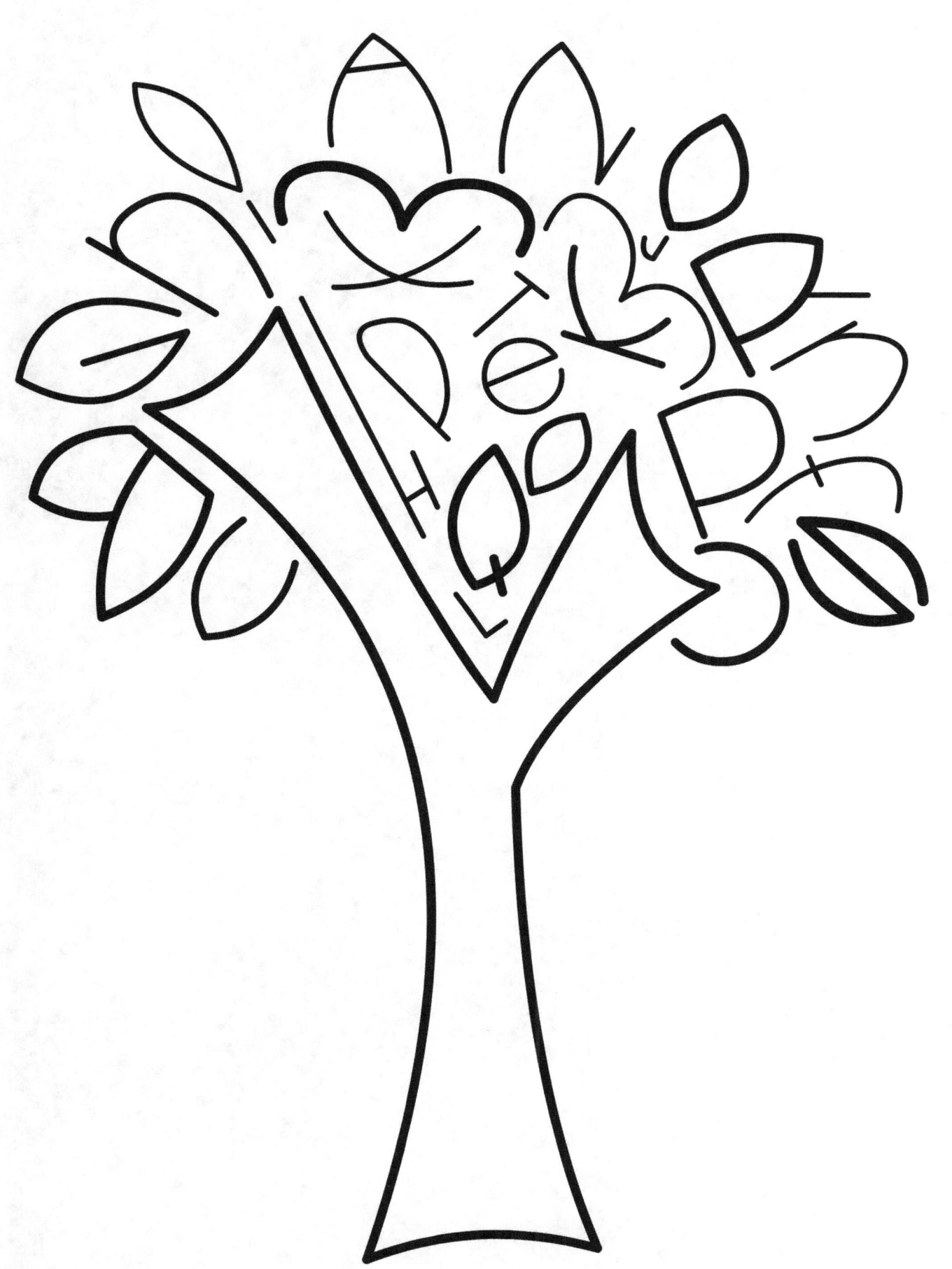

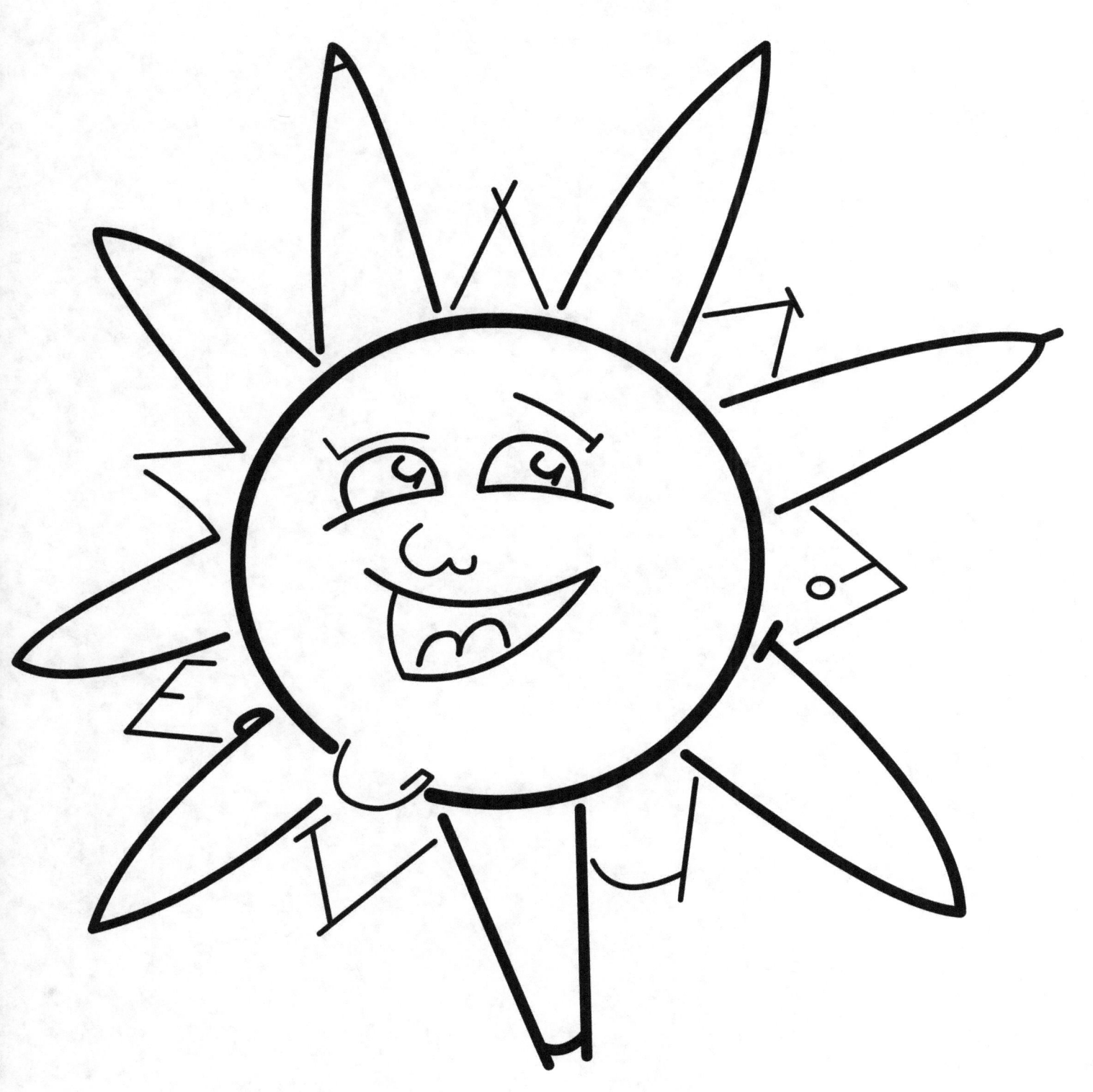

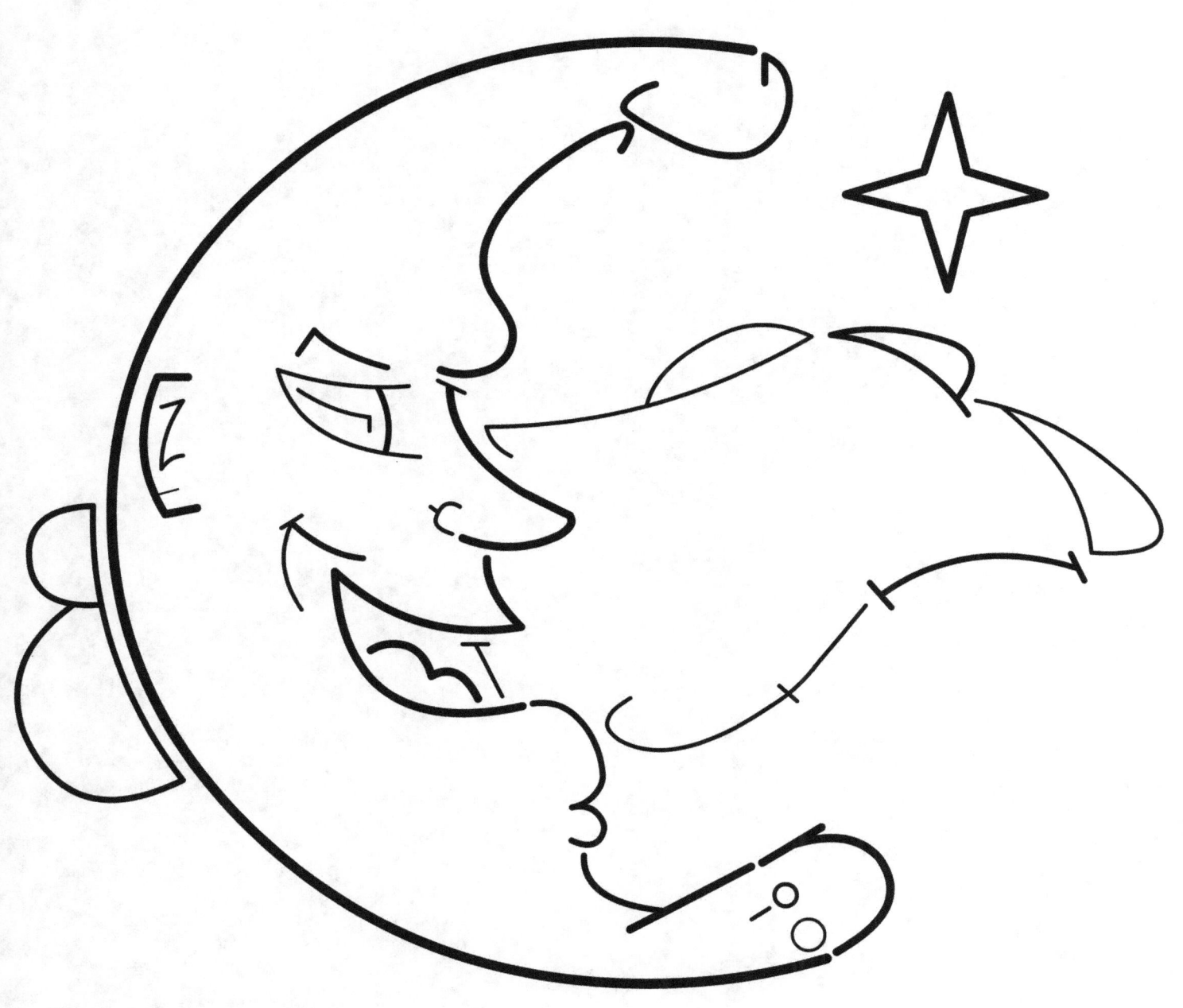

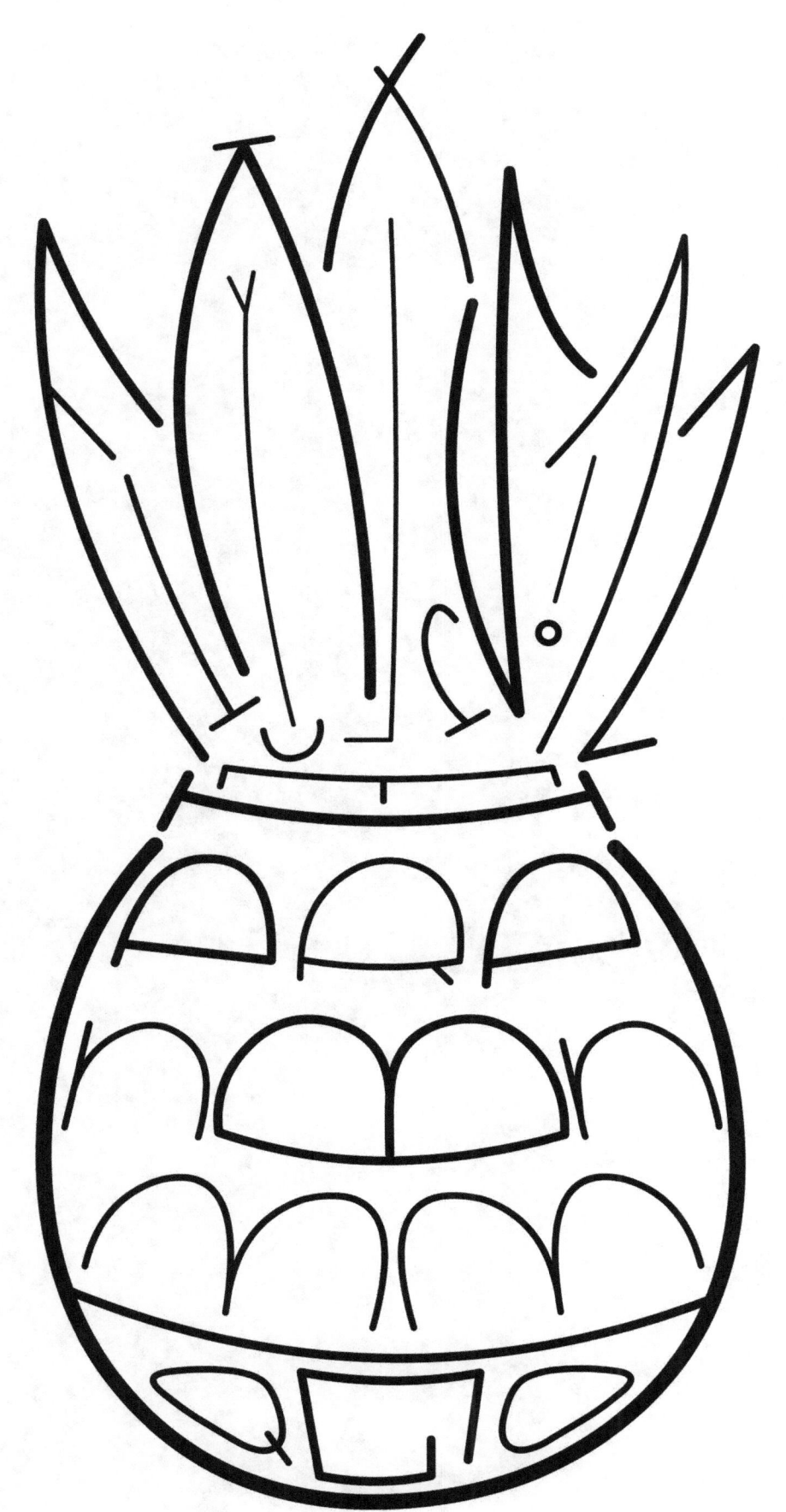

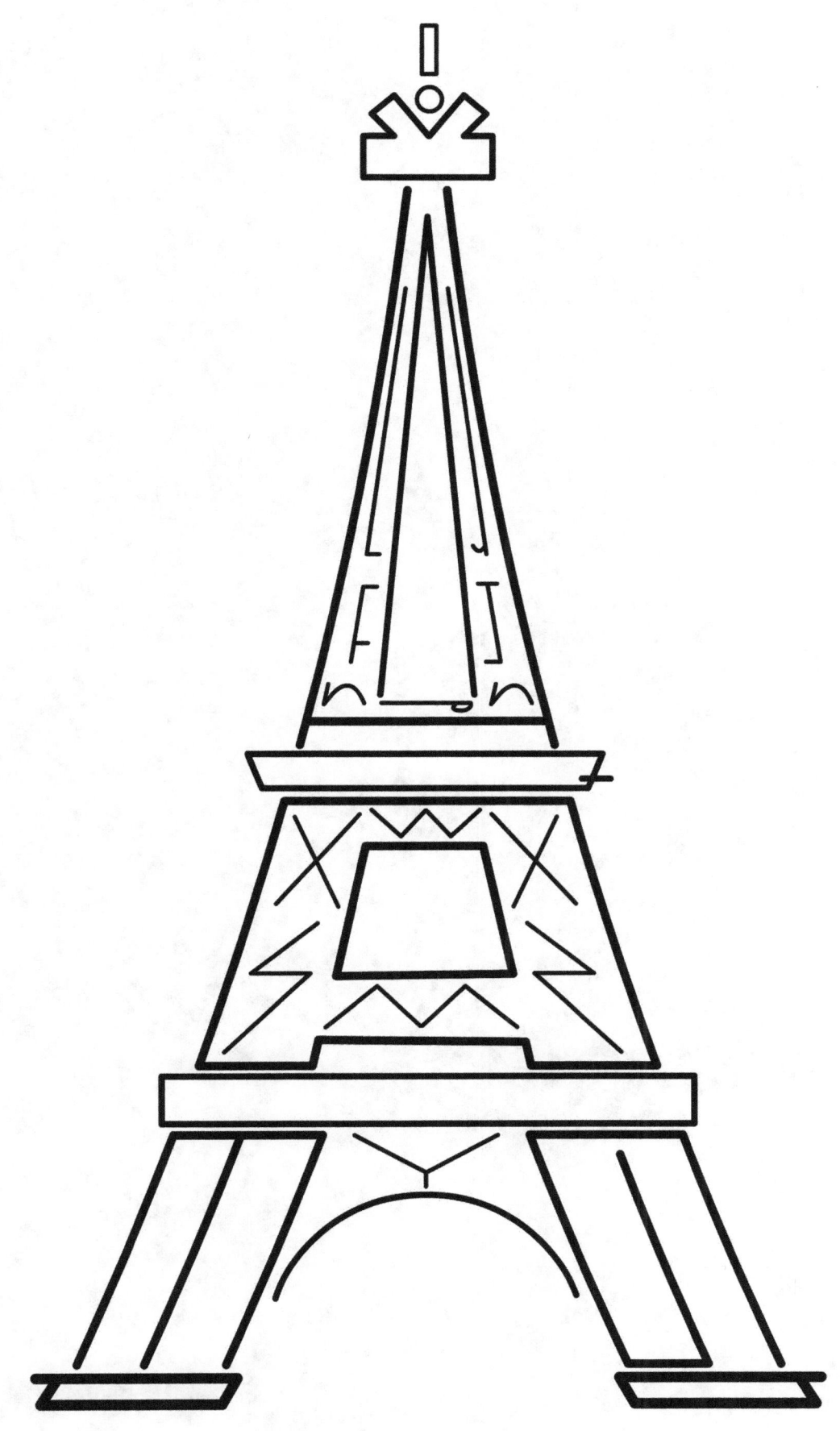

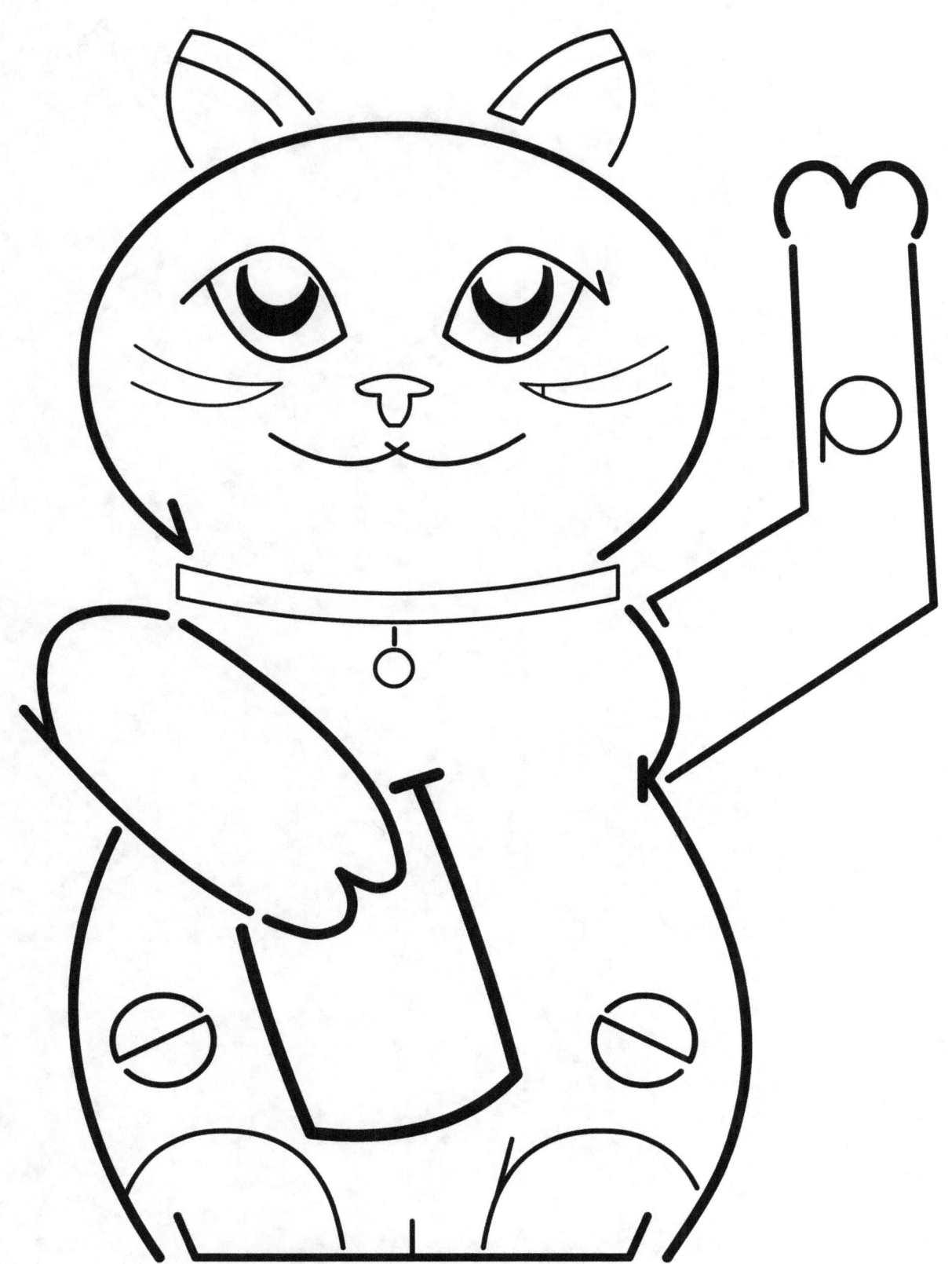

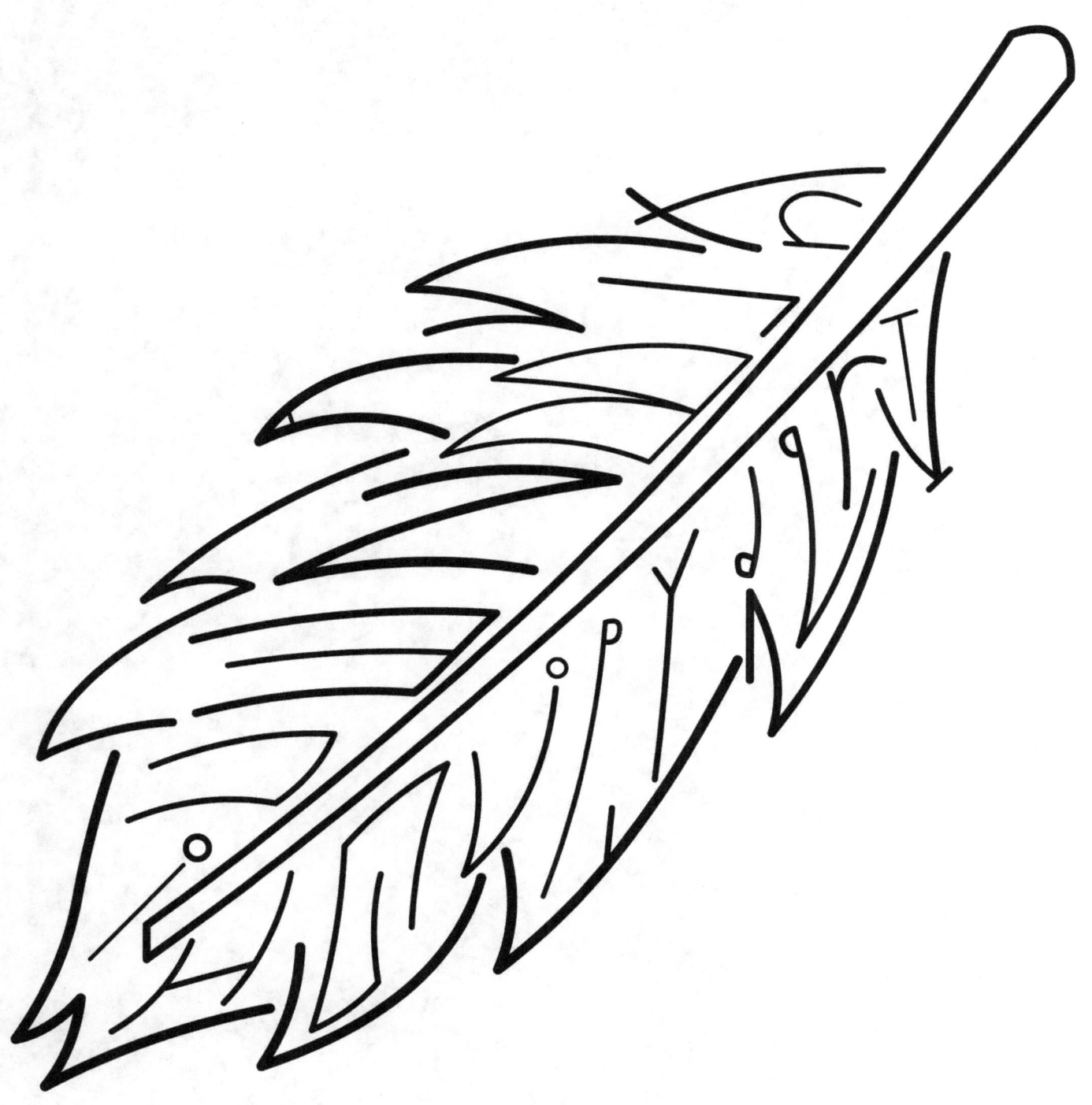

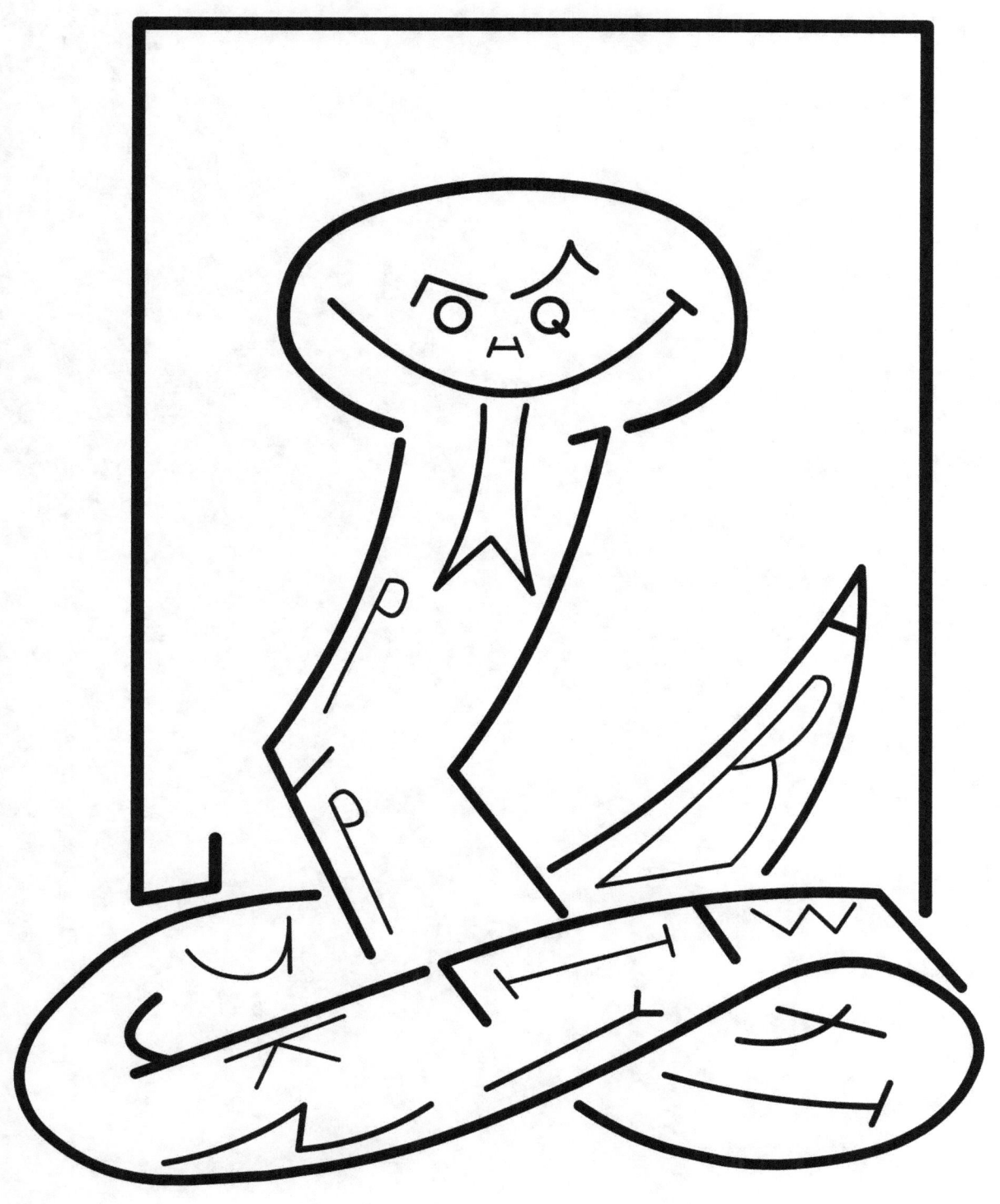

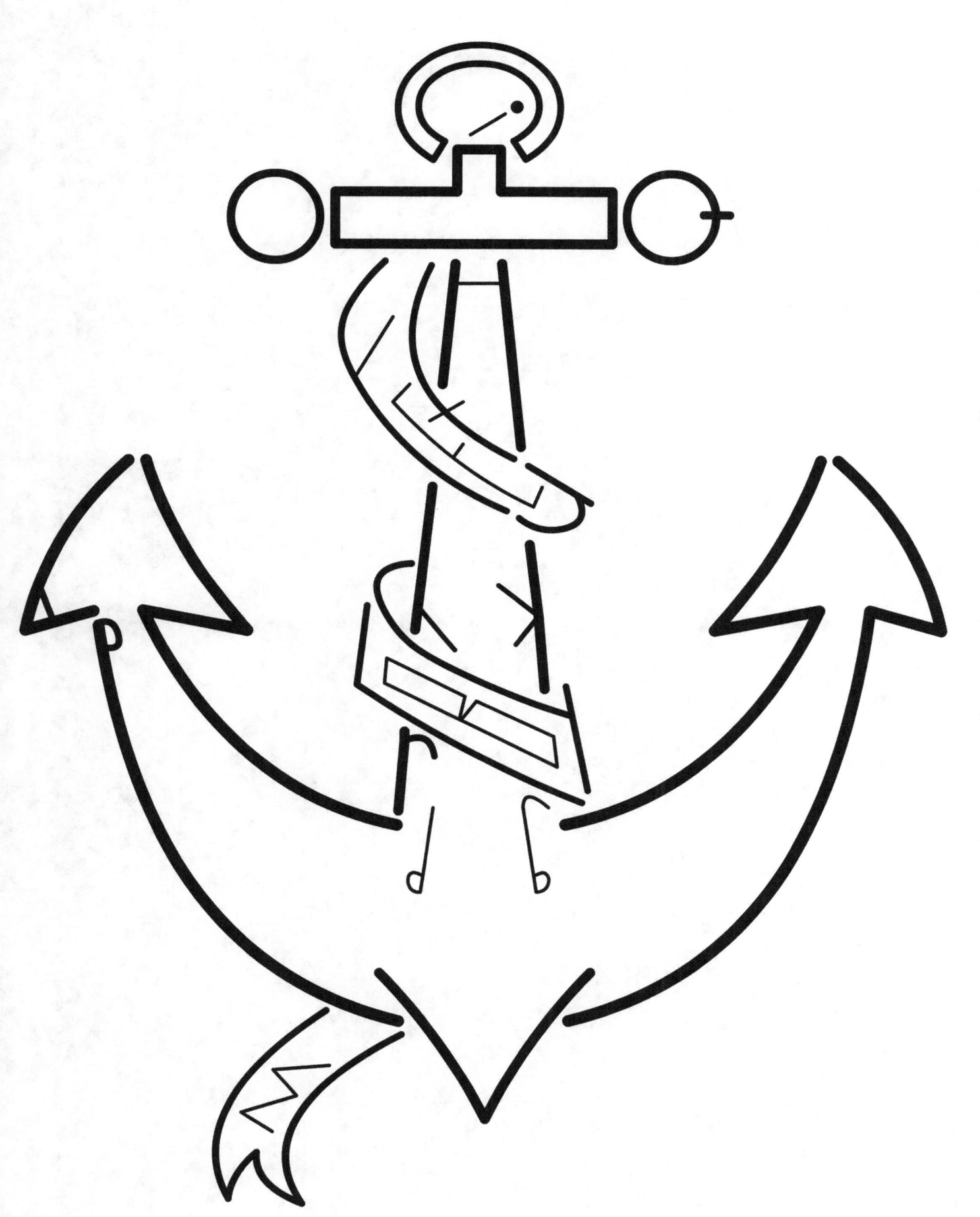

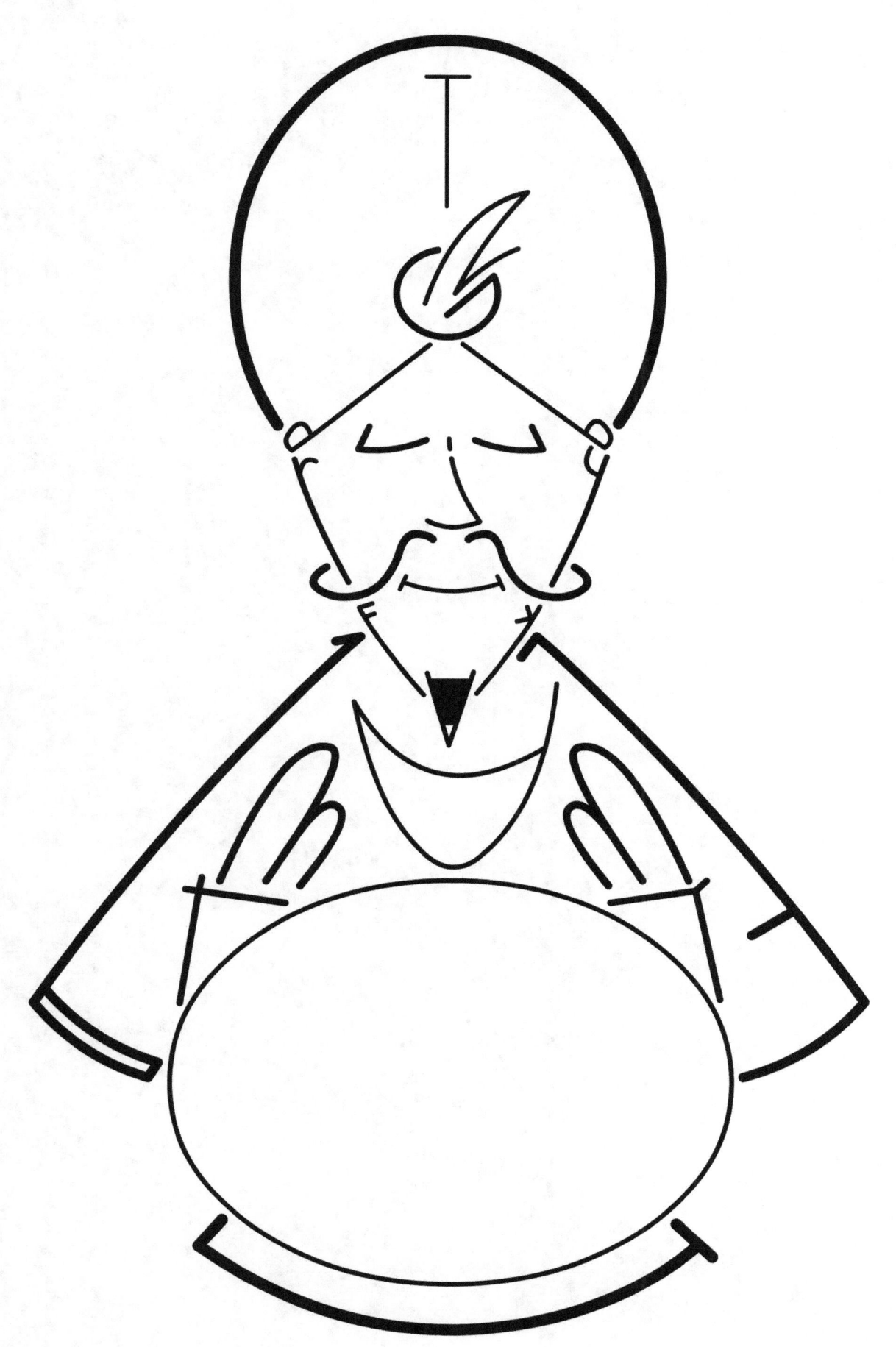

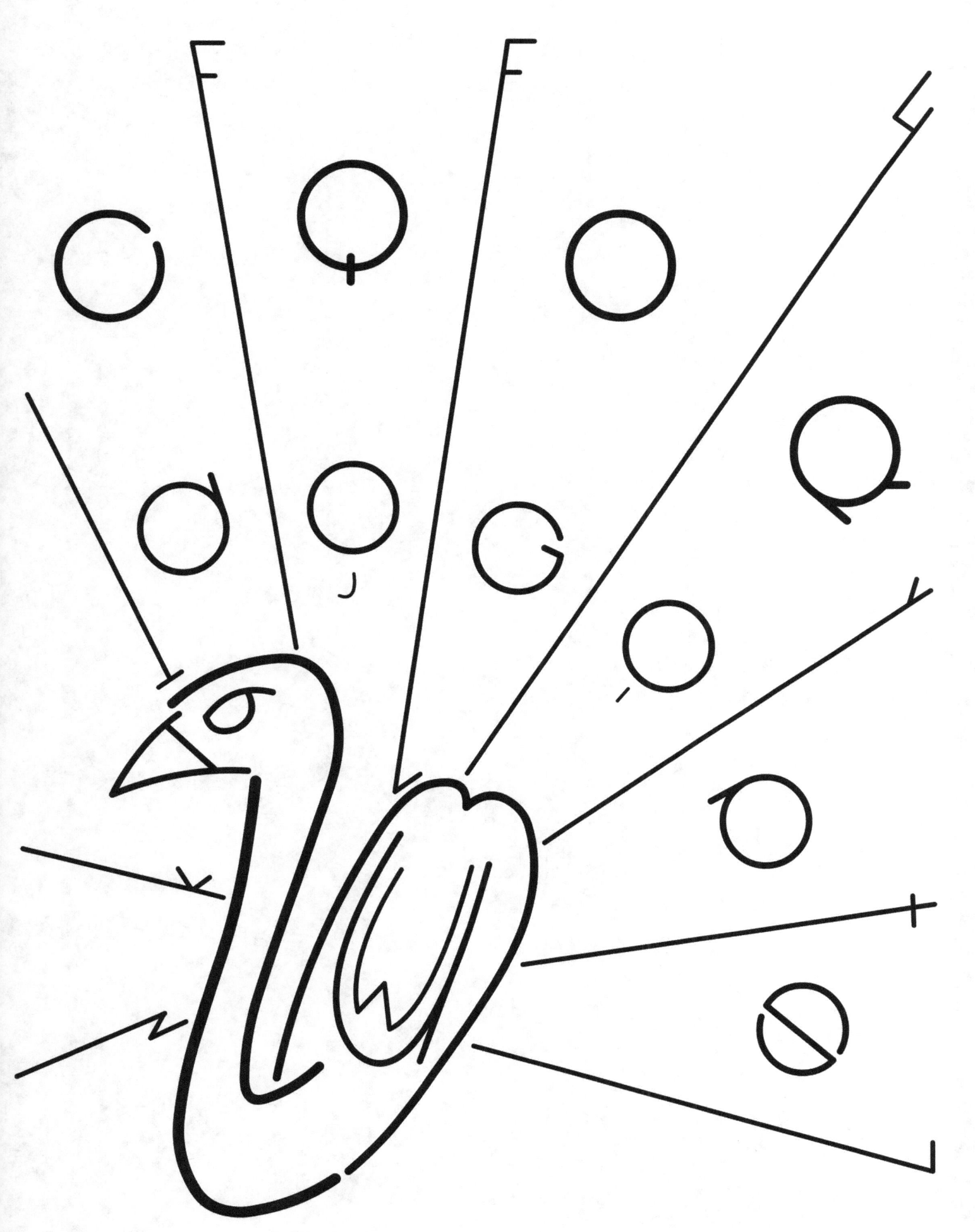

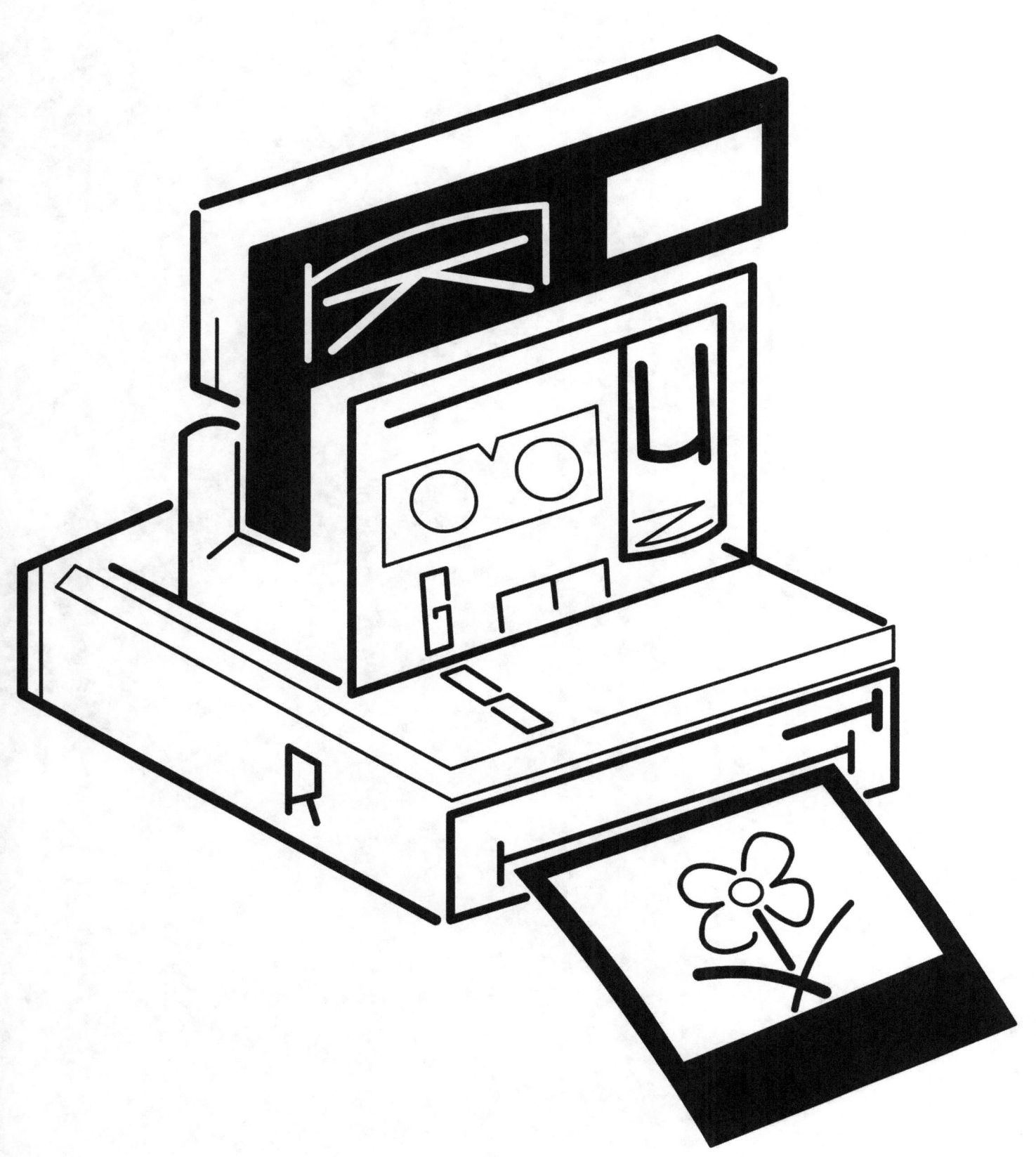

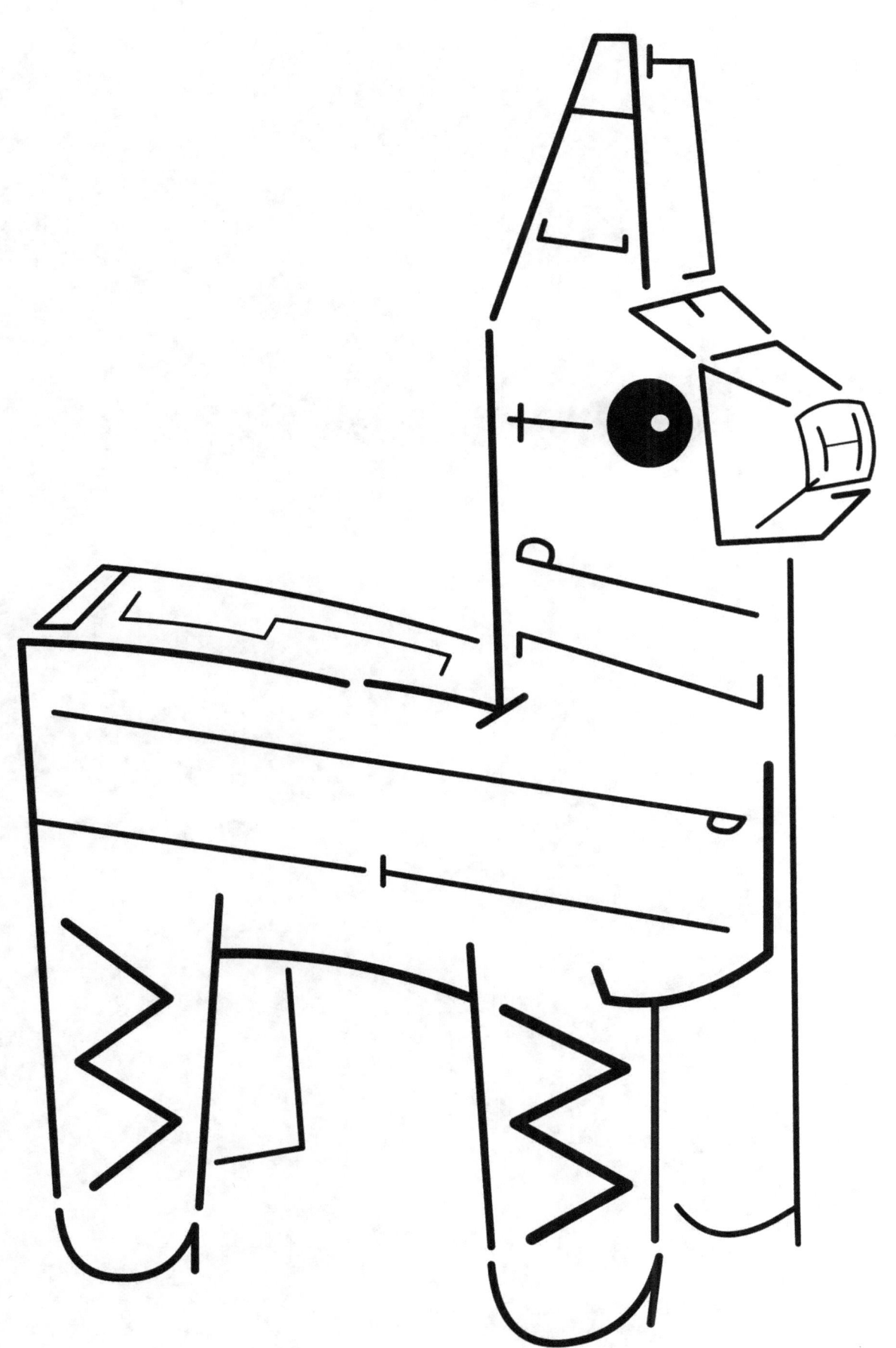

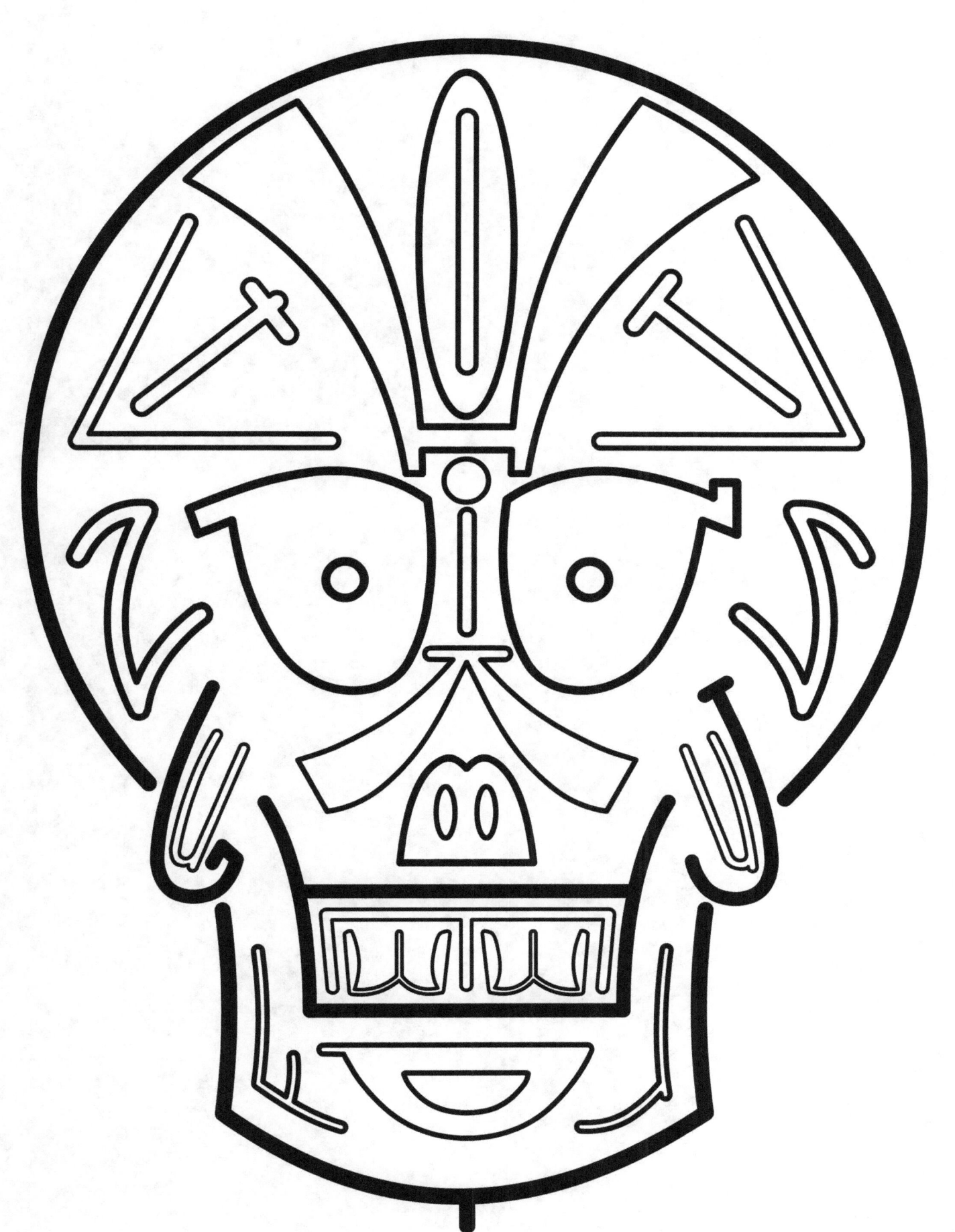

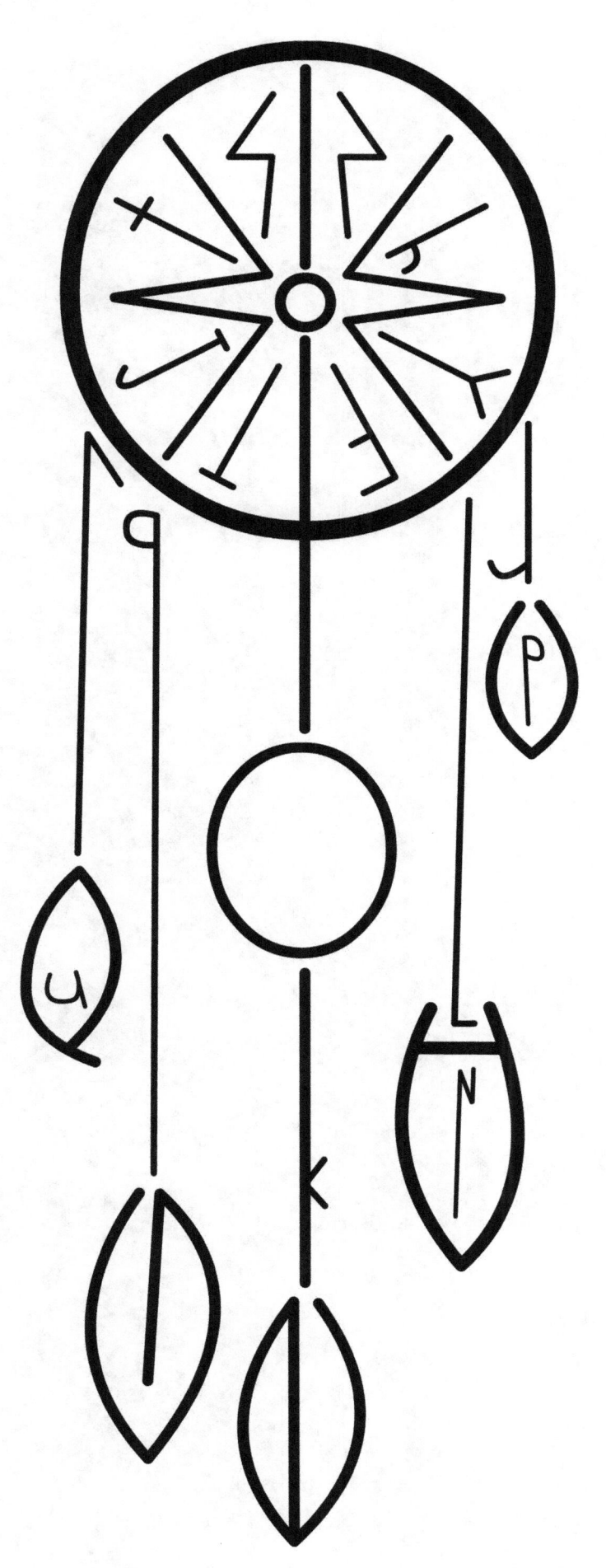

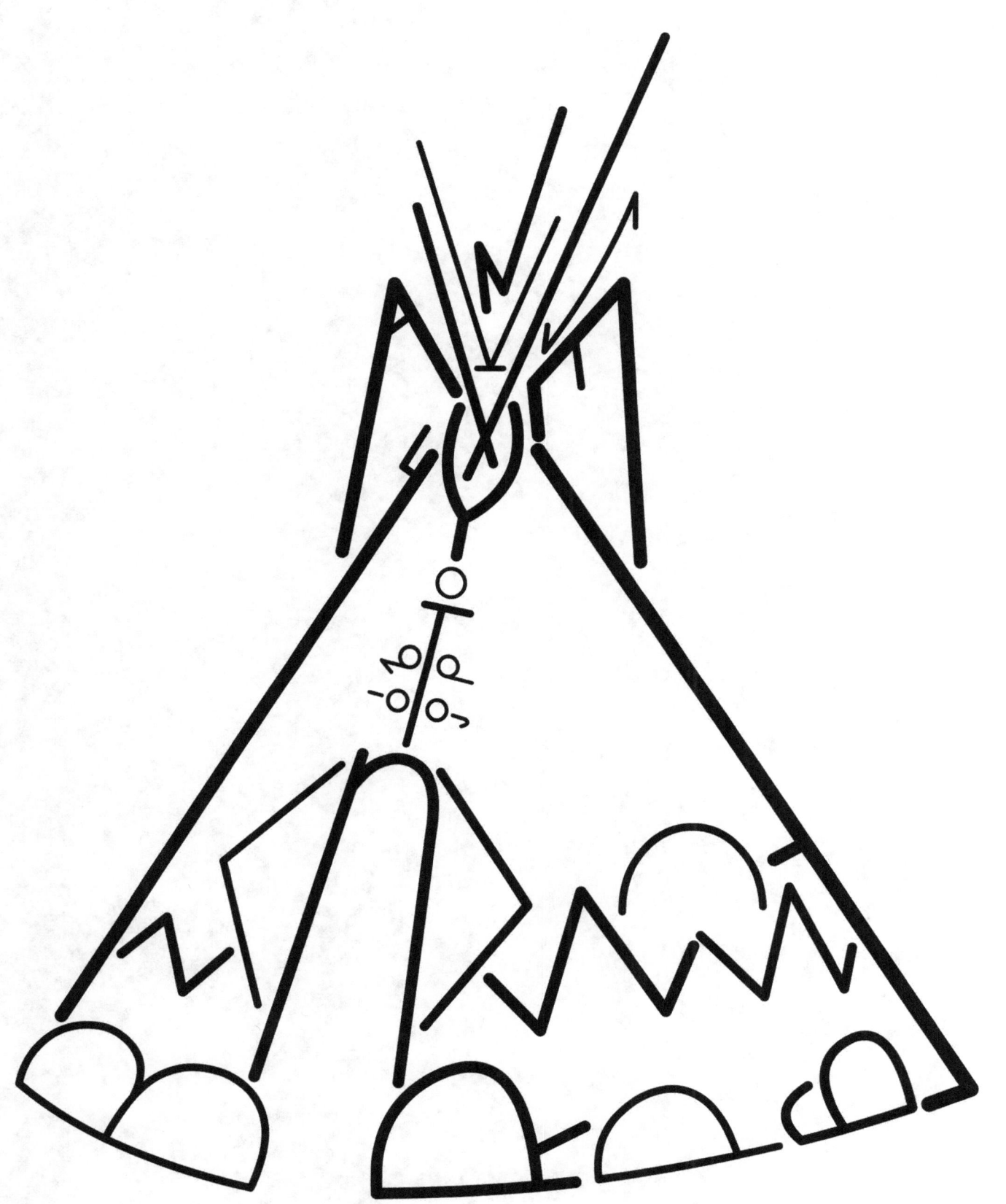

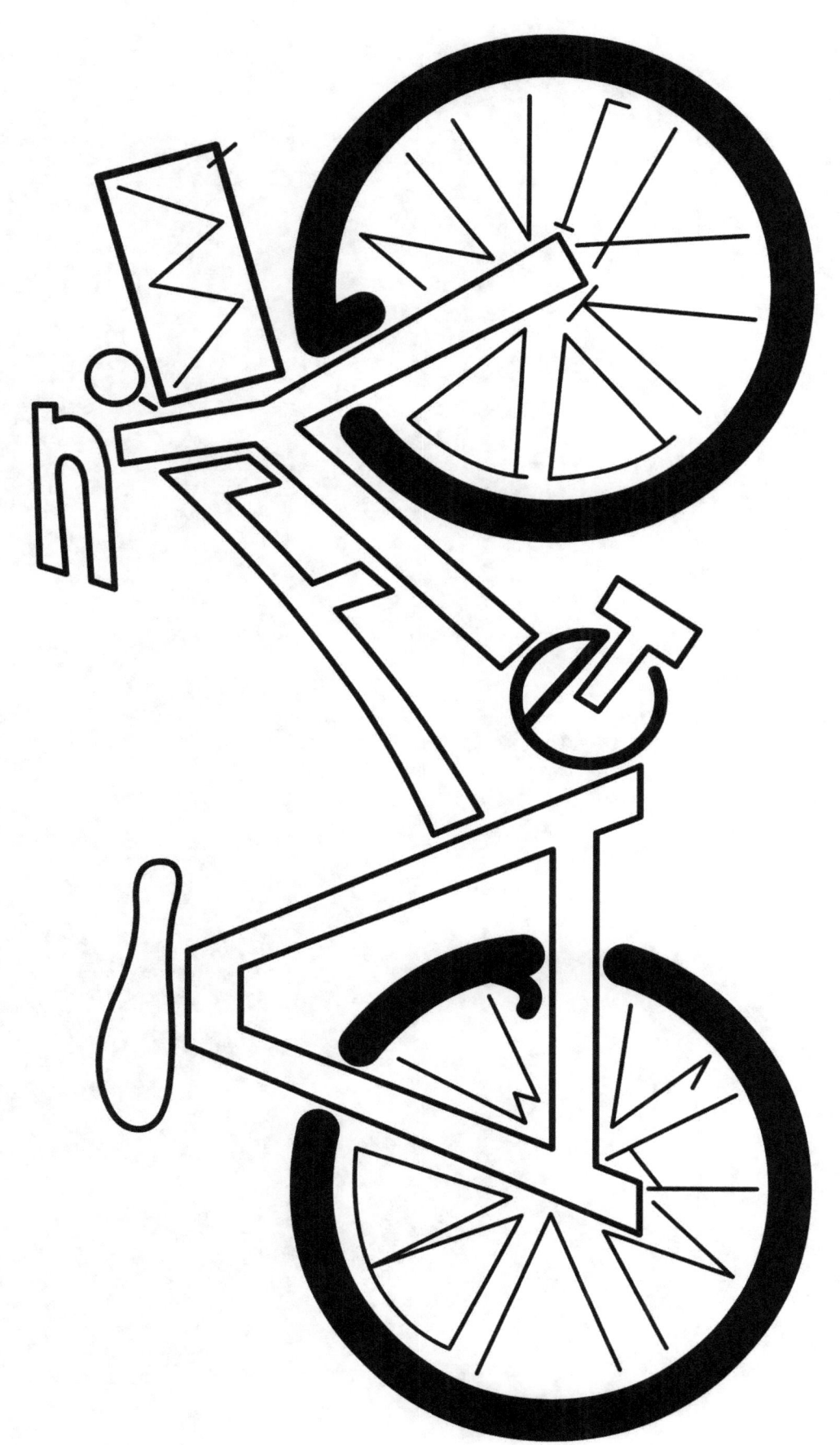

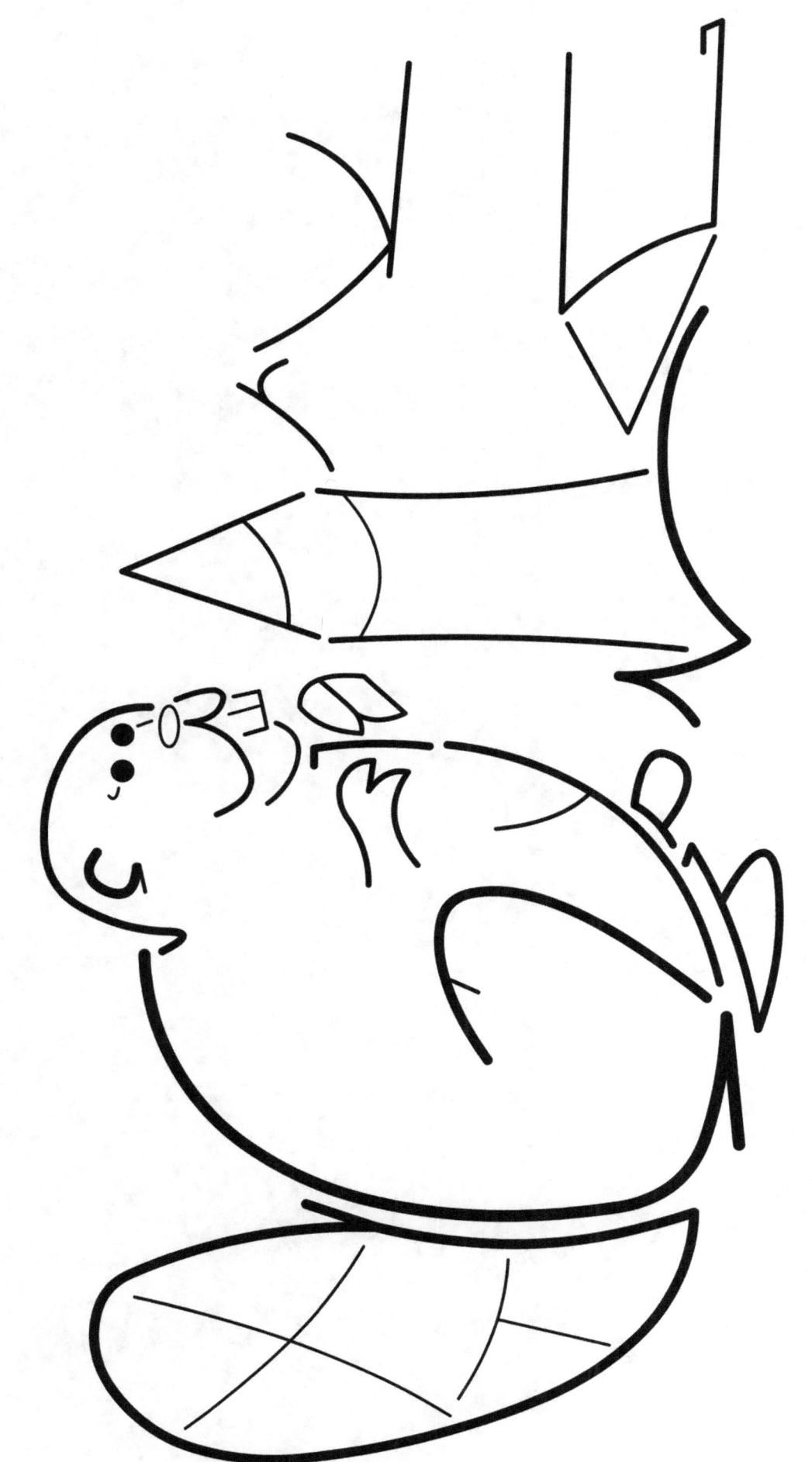

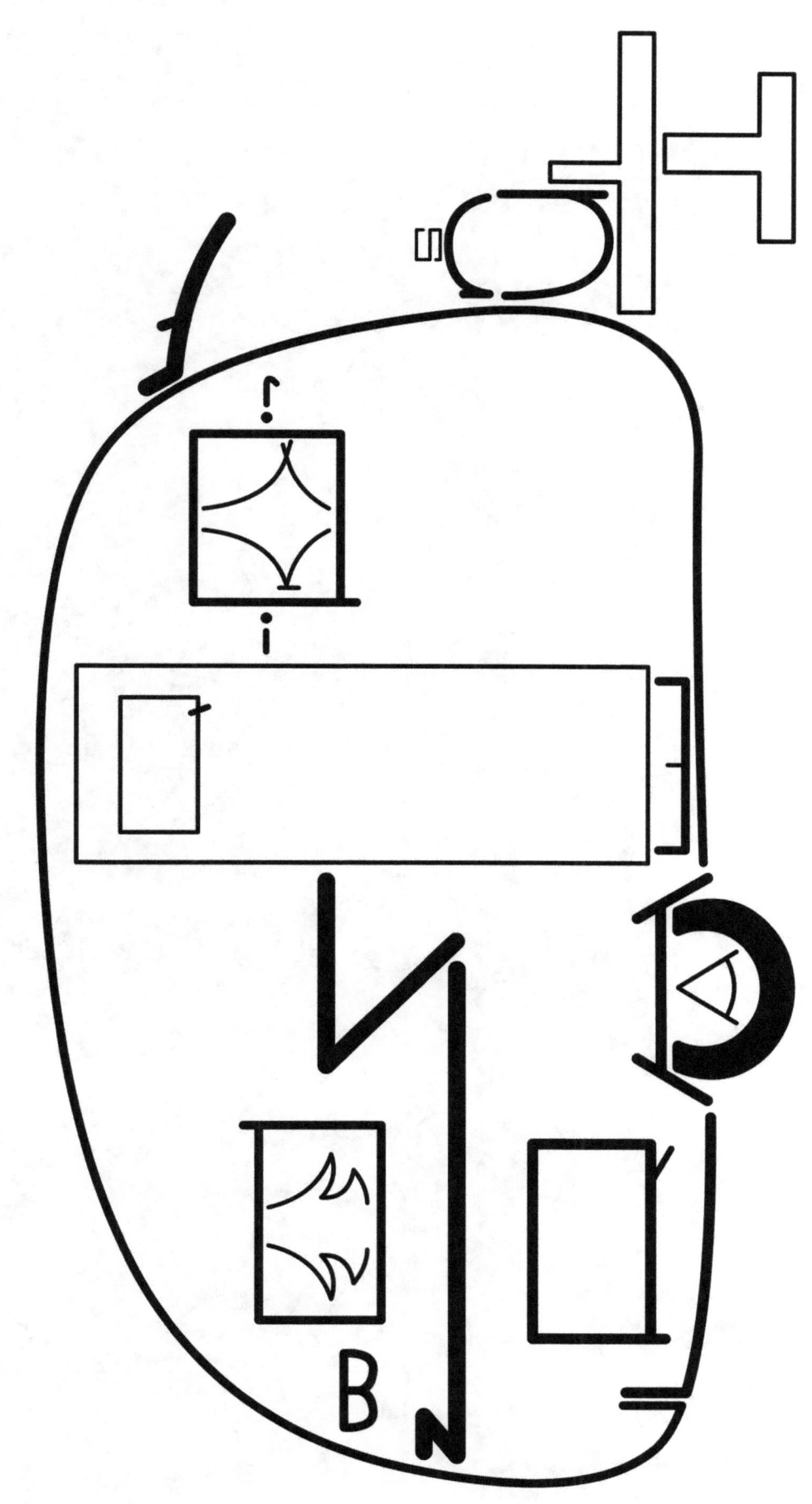

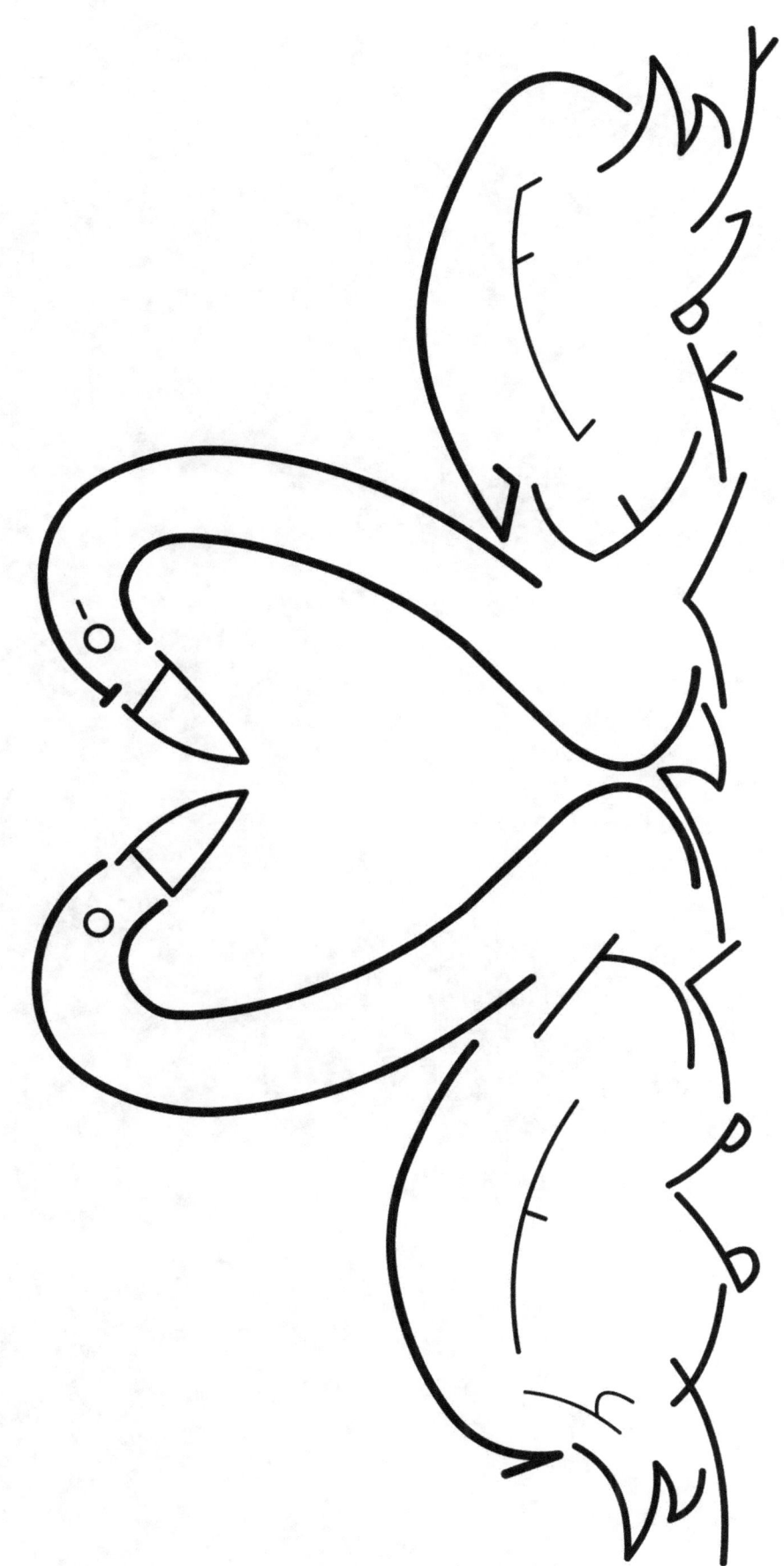

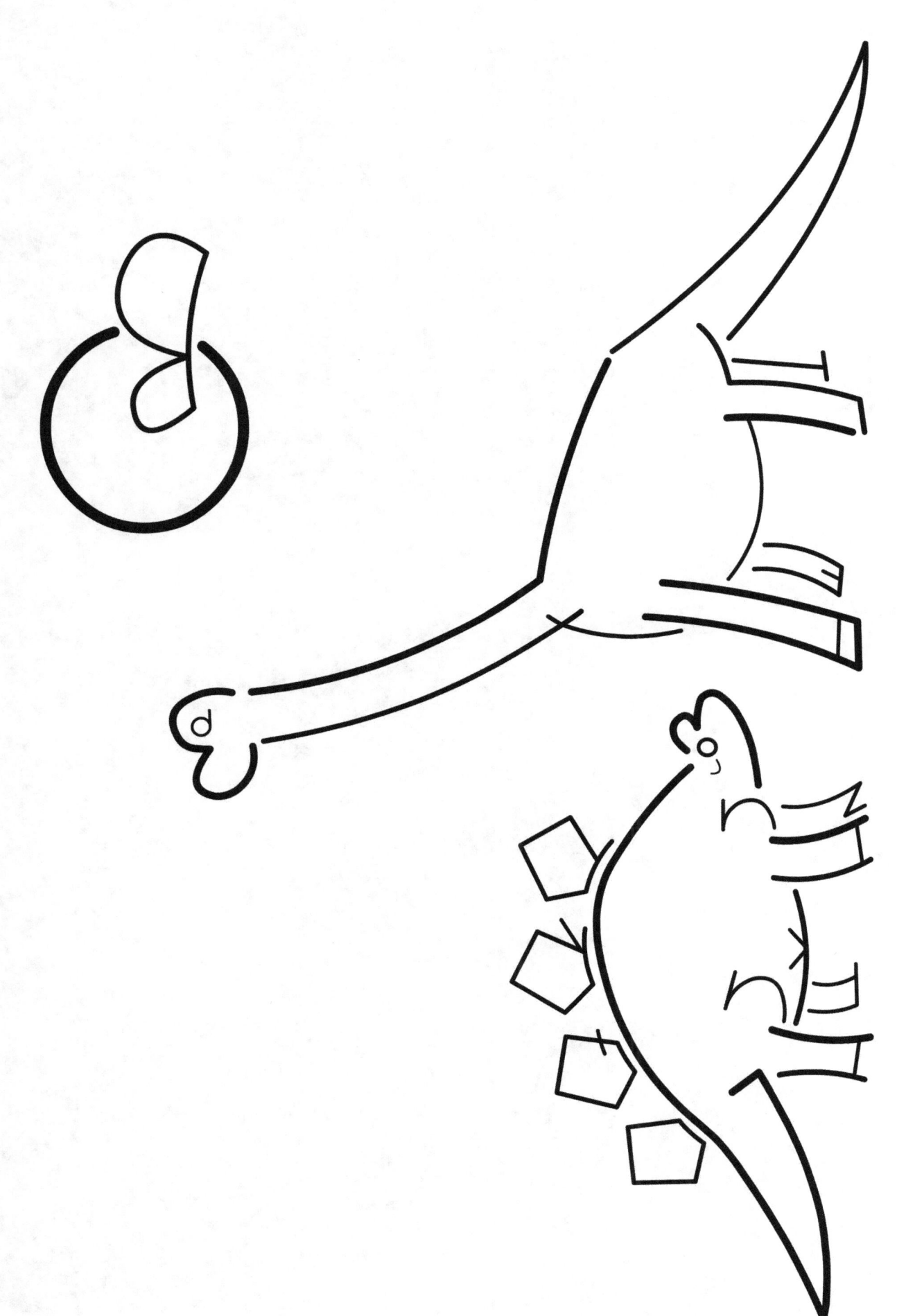

Letter Locations!

Each letter of the alphabet appears in the art once in either lower or upper case. The letters may be stretched, skewed, or rotated. In some instances, certain letters could be considered interchangeable due to their natural construction (ex. M is W upside down).

Letter interchangeability could involve: d & p; H & I; L & V; M & W; n & u; N & Z; x & t; Y & T.

Consider this goat.

His pupils are identical. One is "u" and the other "n." They are interchangeable. The "L" is found in his ear while the "V" is his horn. They are drawn differently enough that they are not interchangeable in this case. In other drawings "L" and "V" may look similar enough to be interchangeable. Interchangeability, if any, varies from image to image.

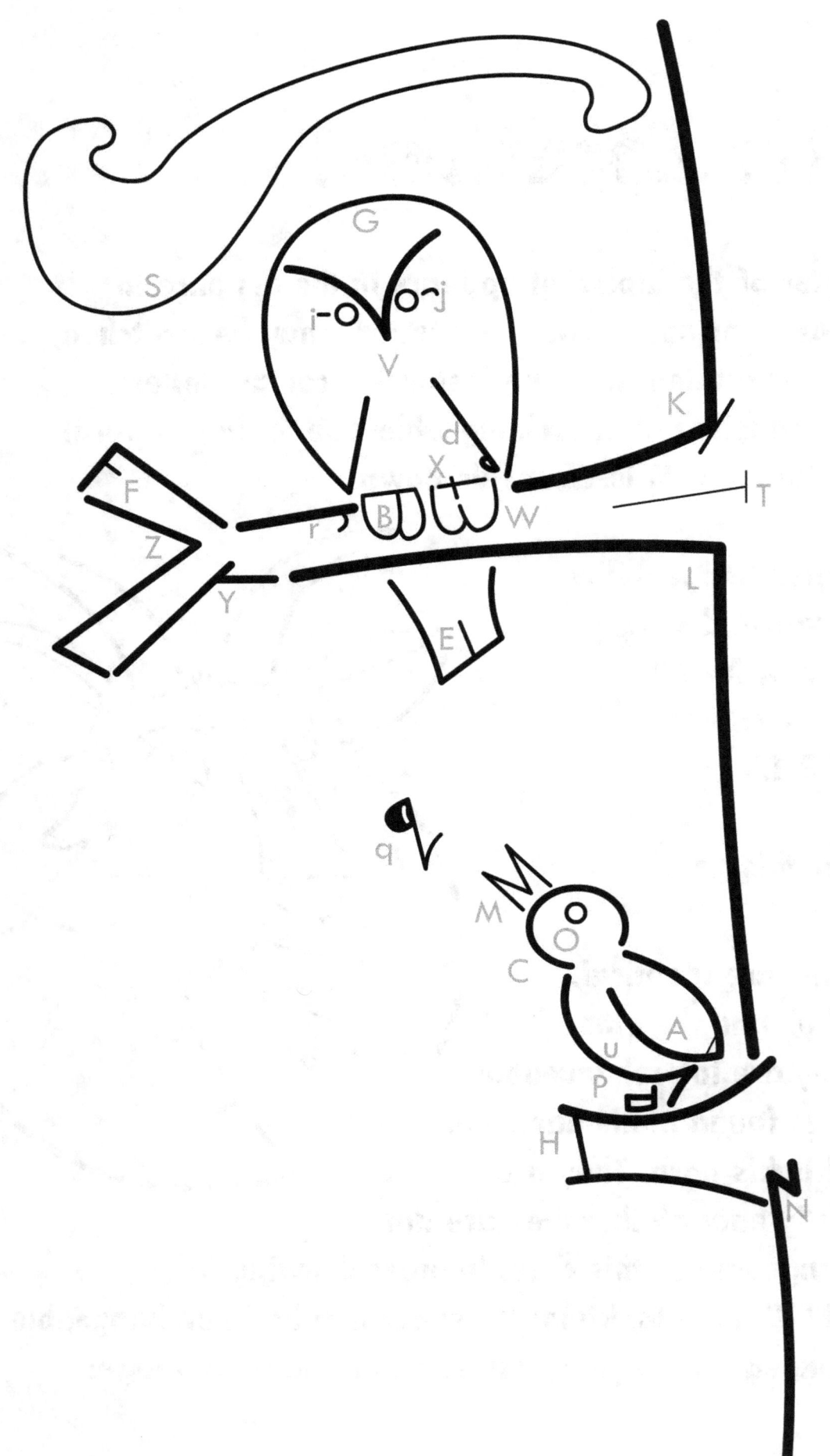

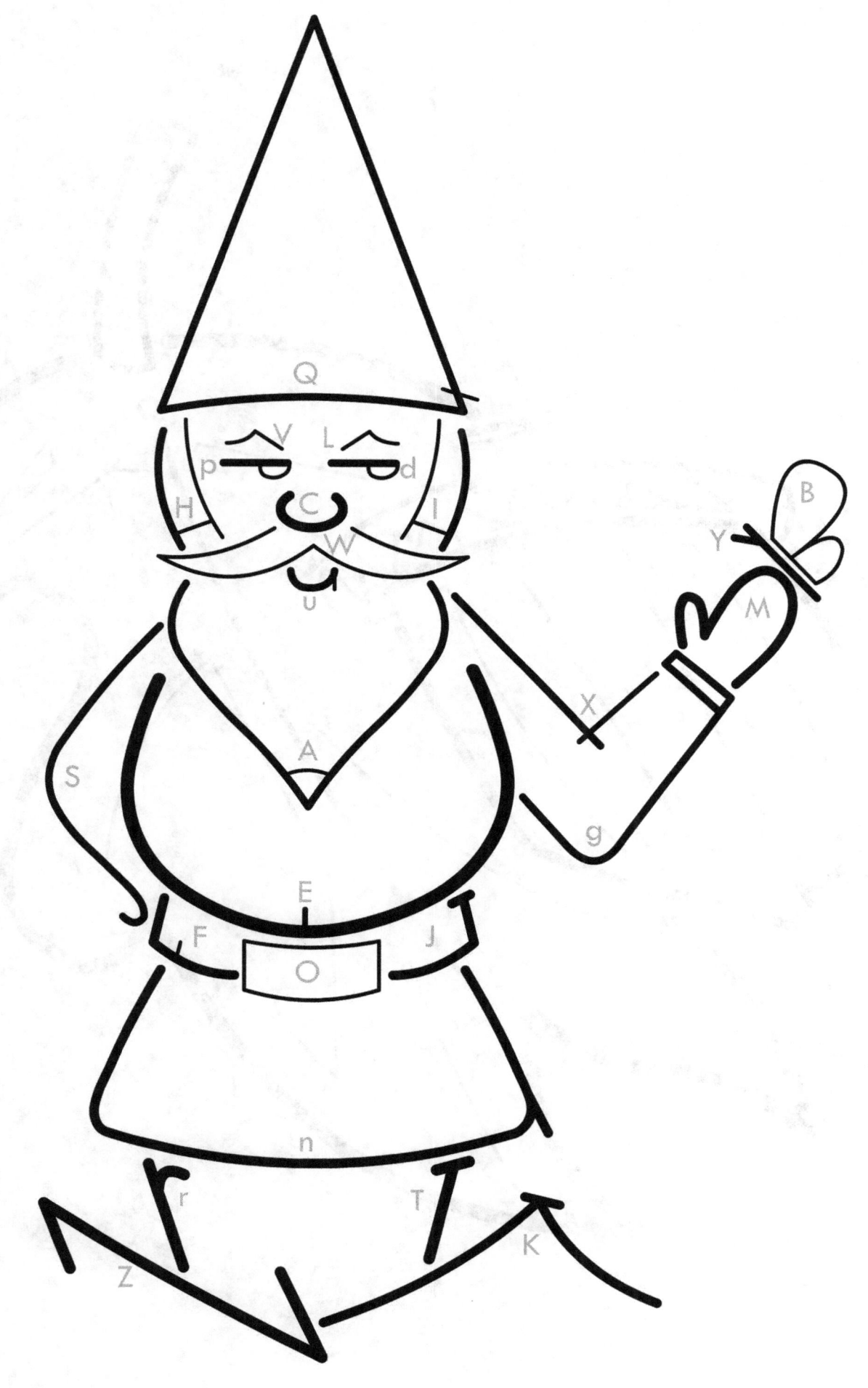

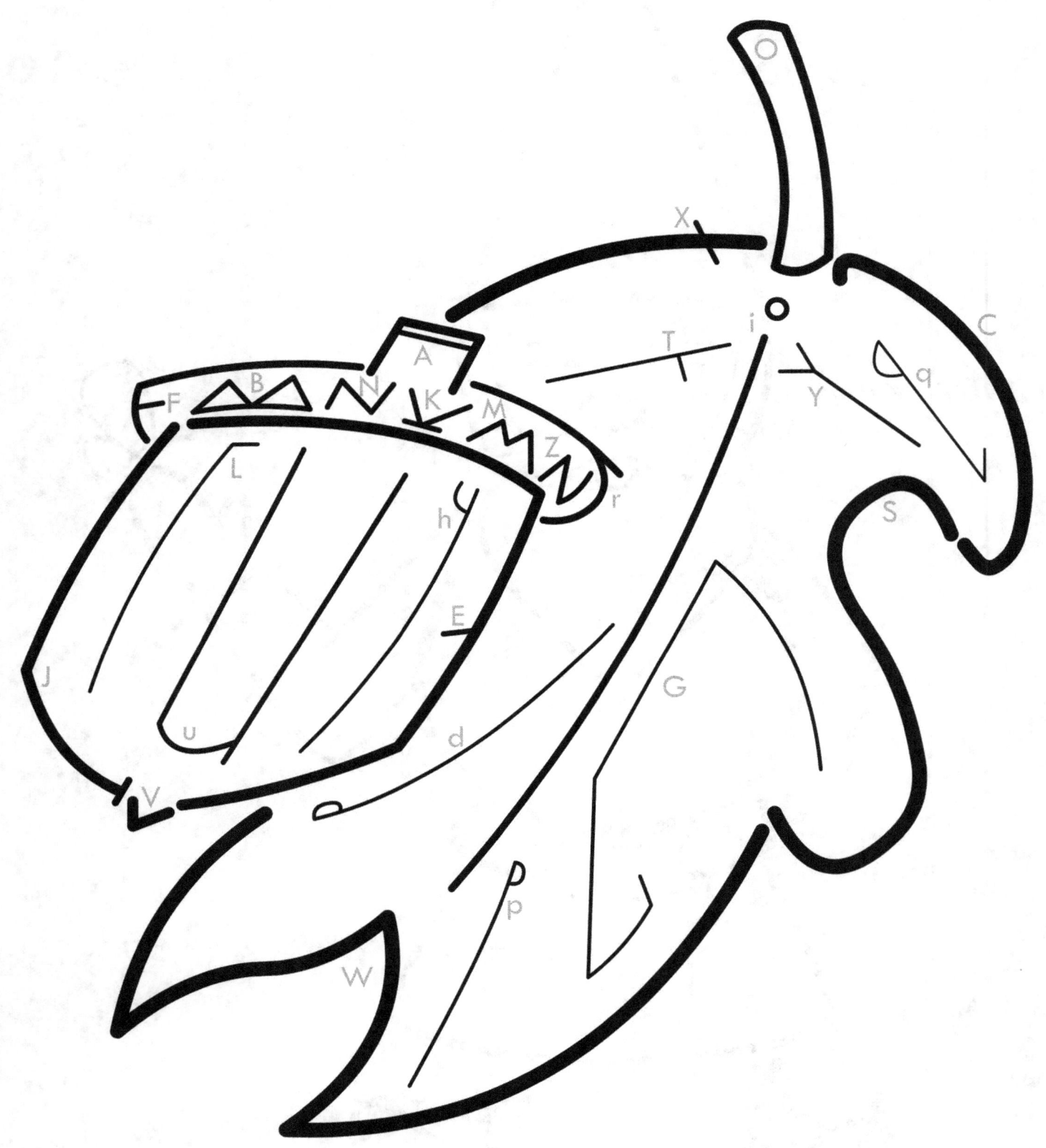

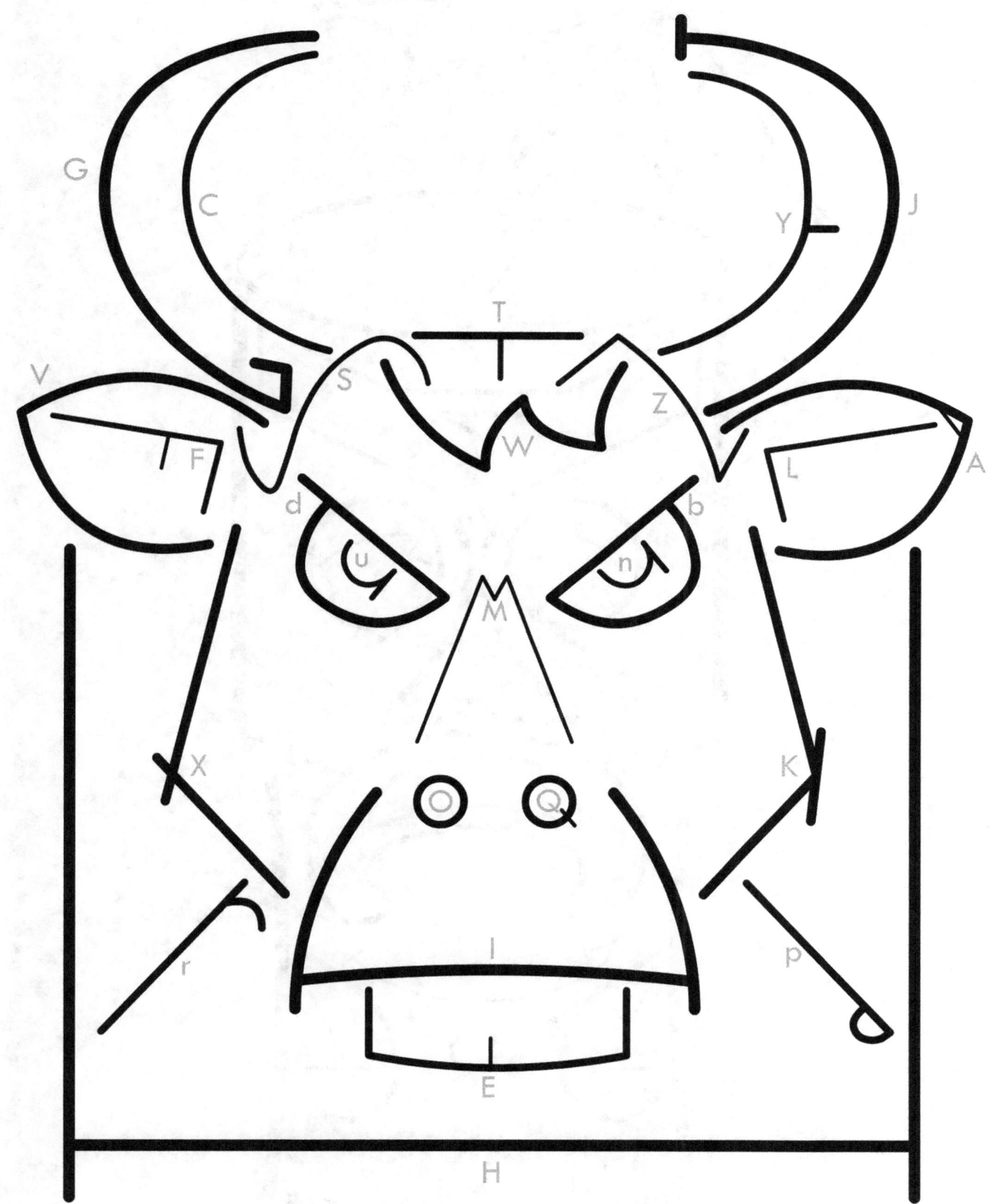

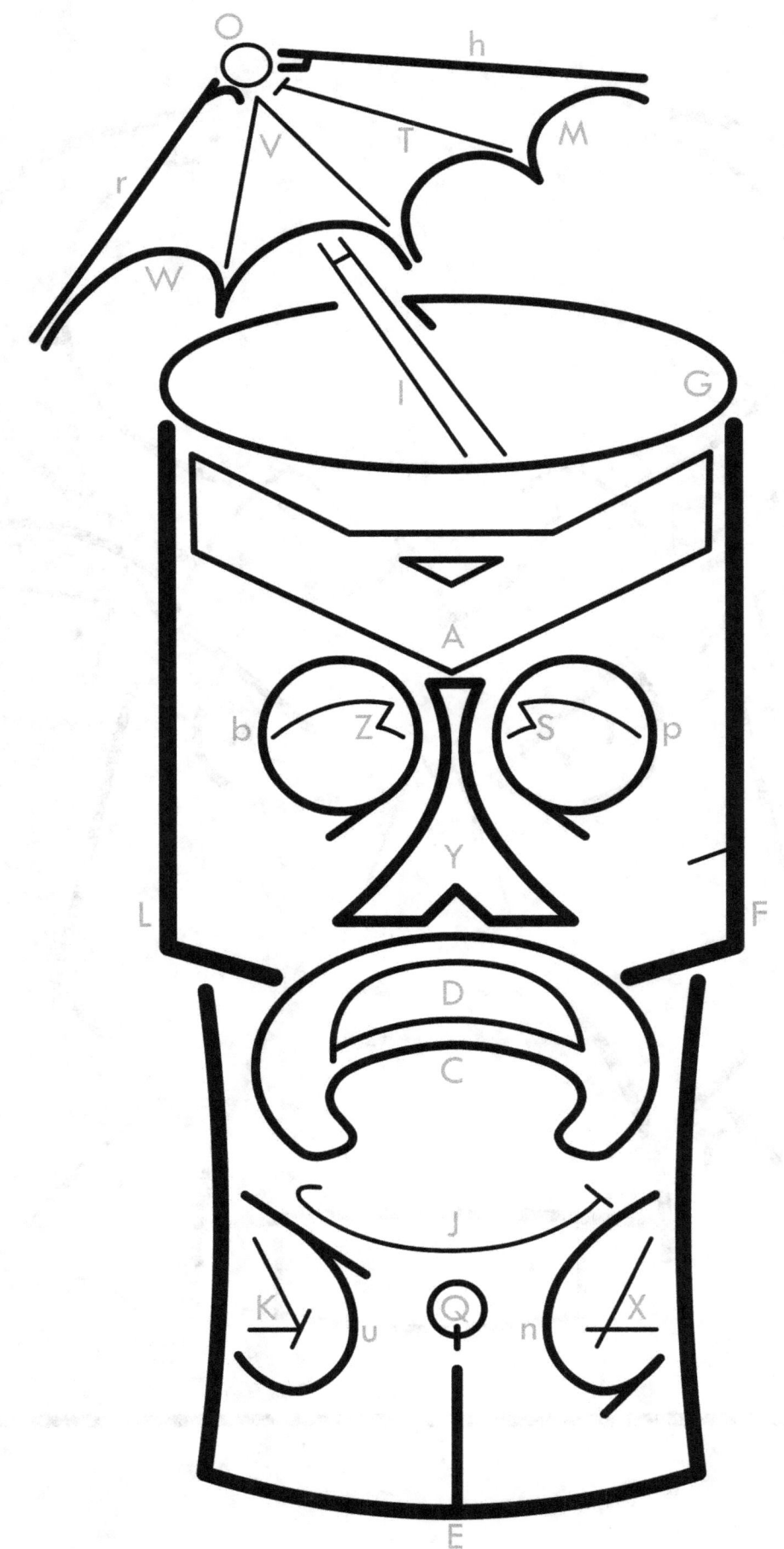

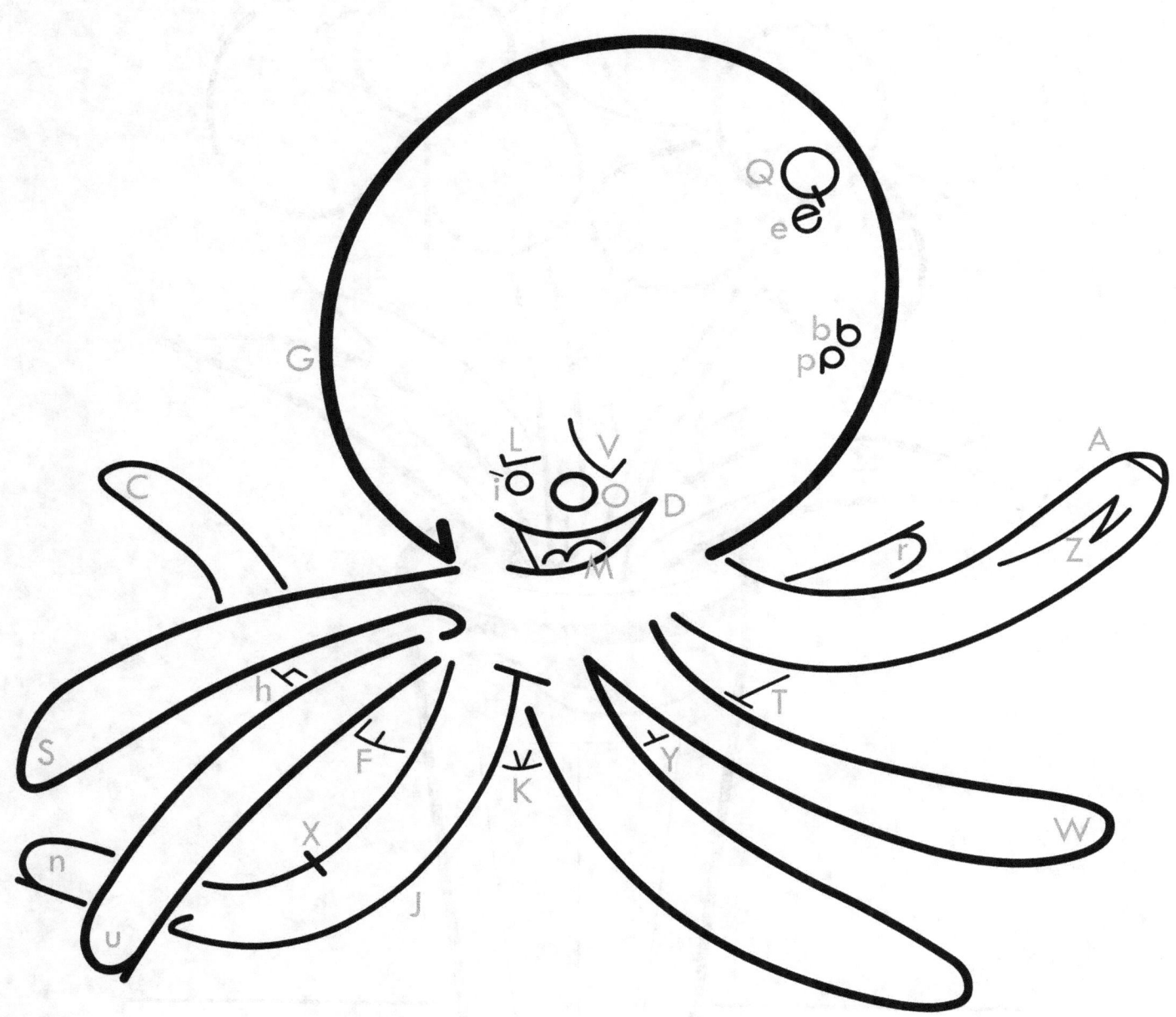

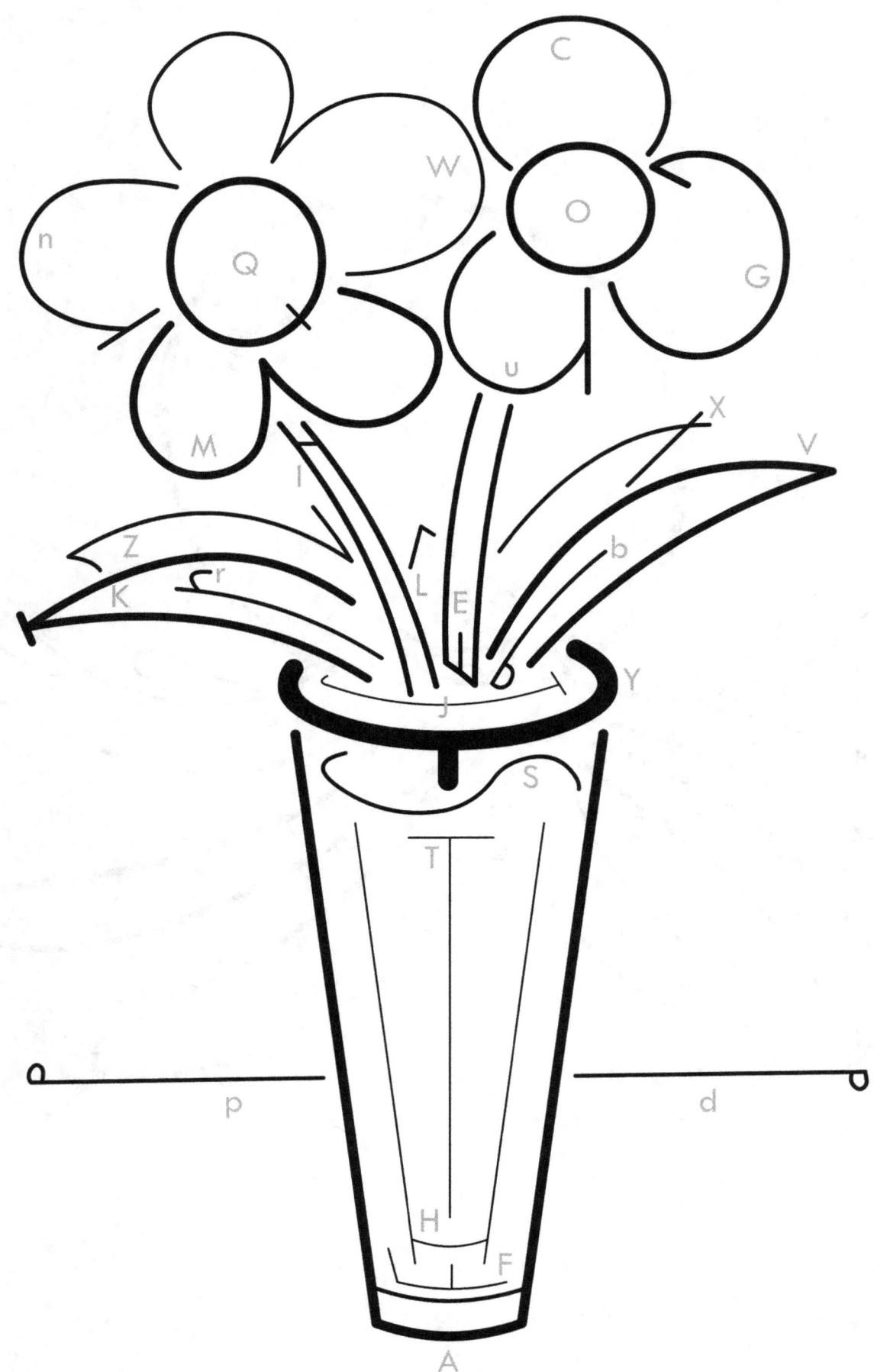

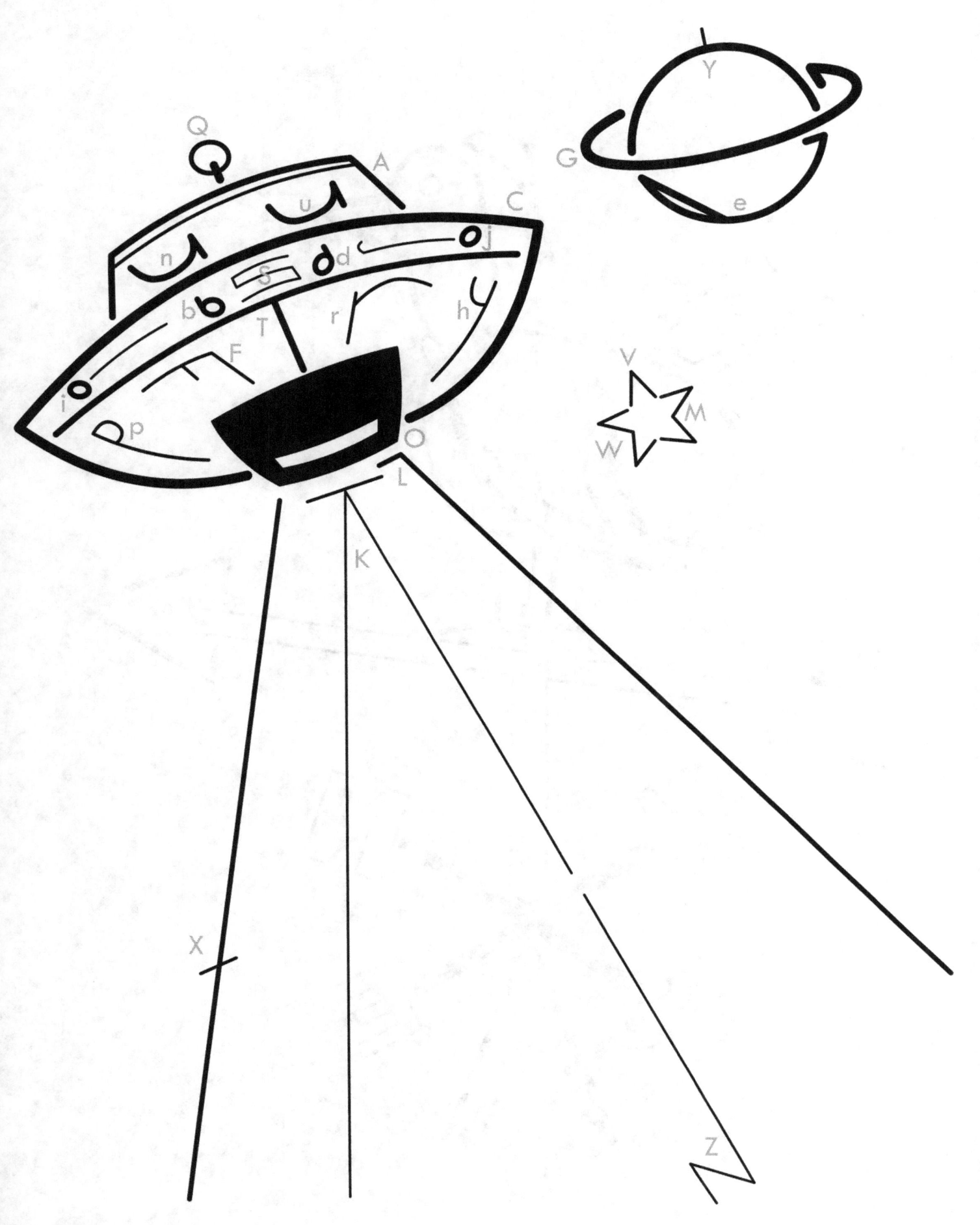

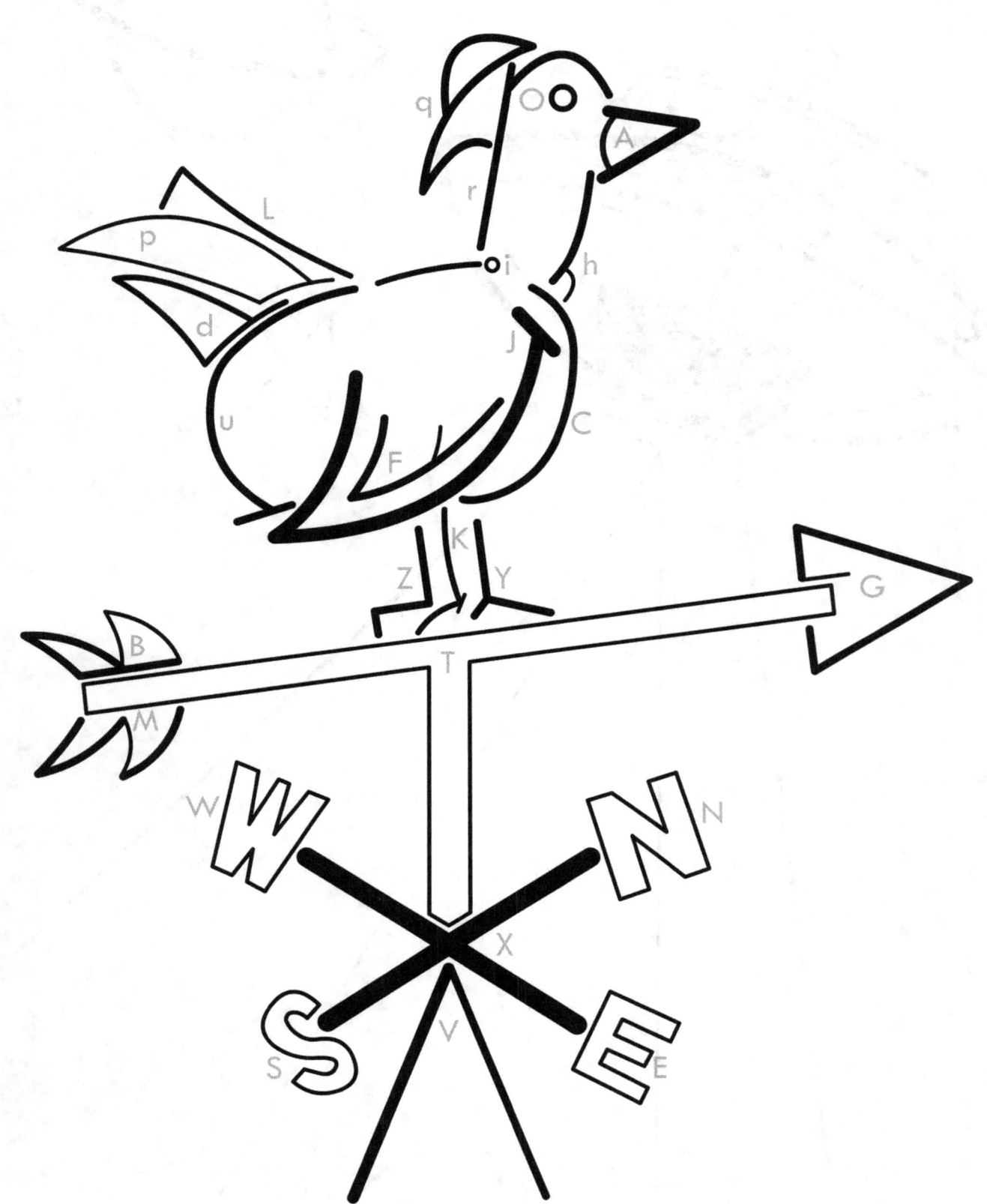

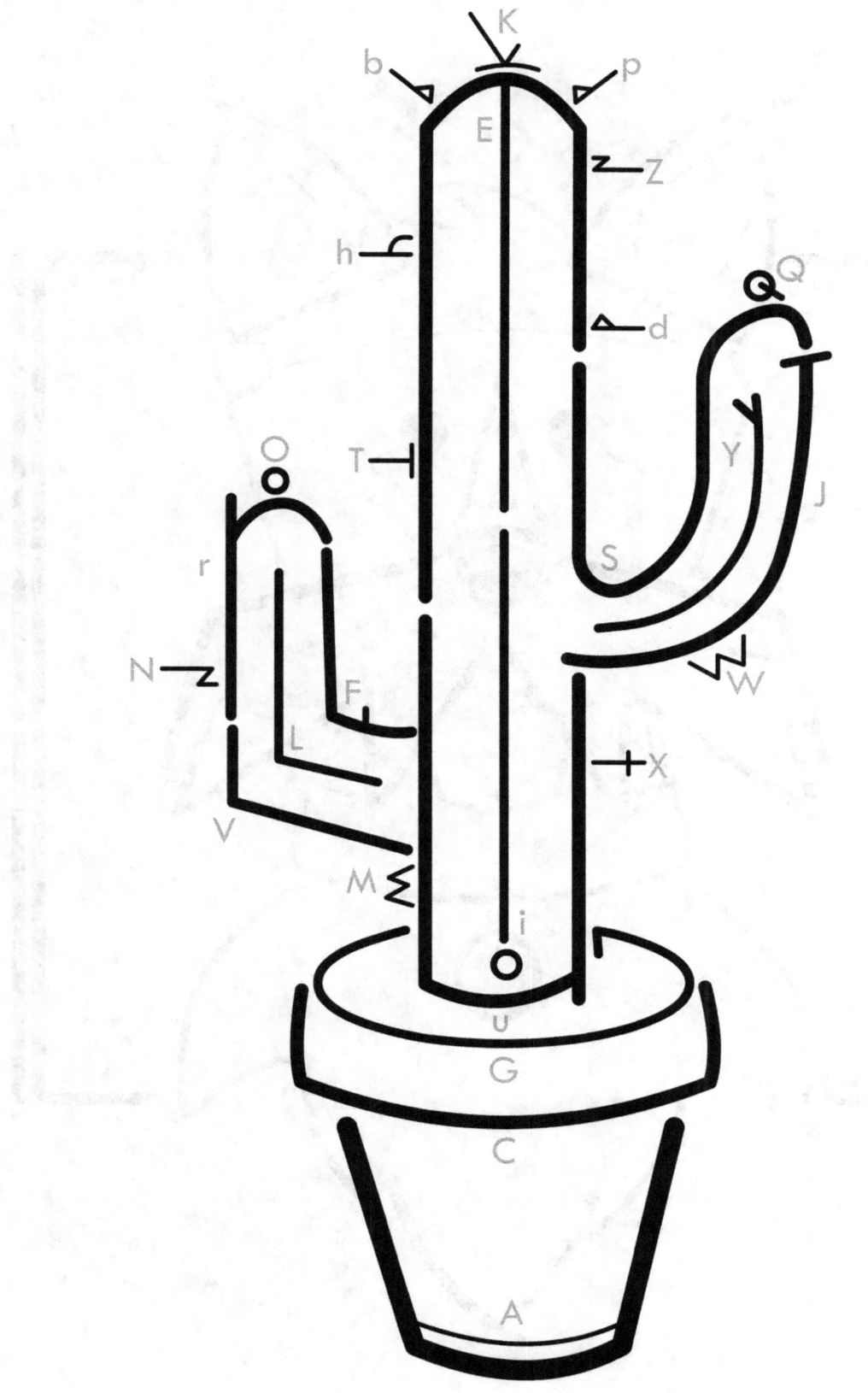

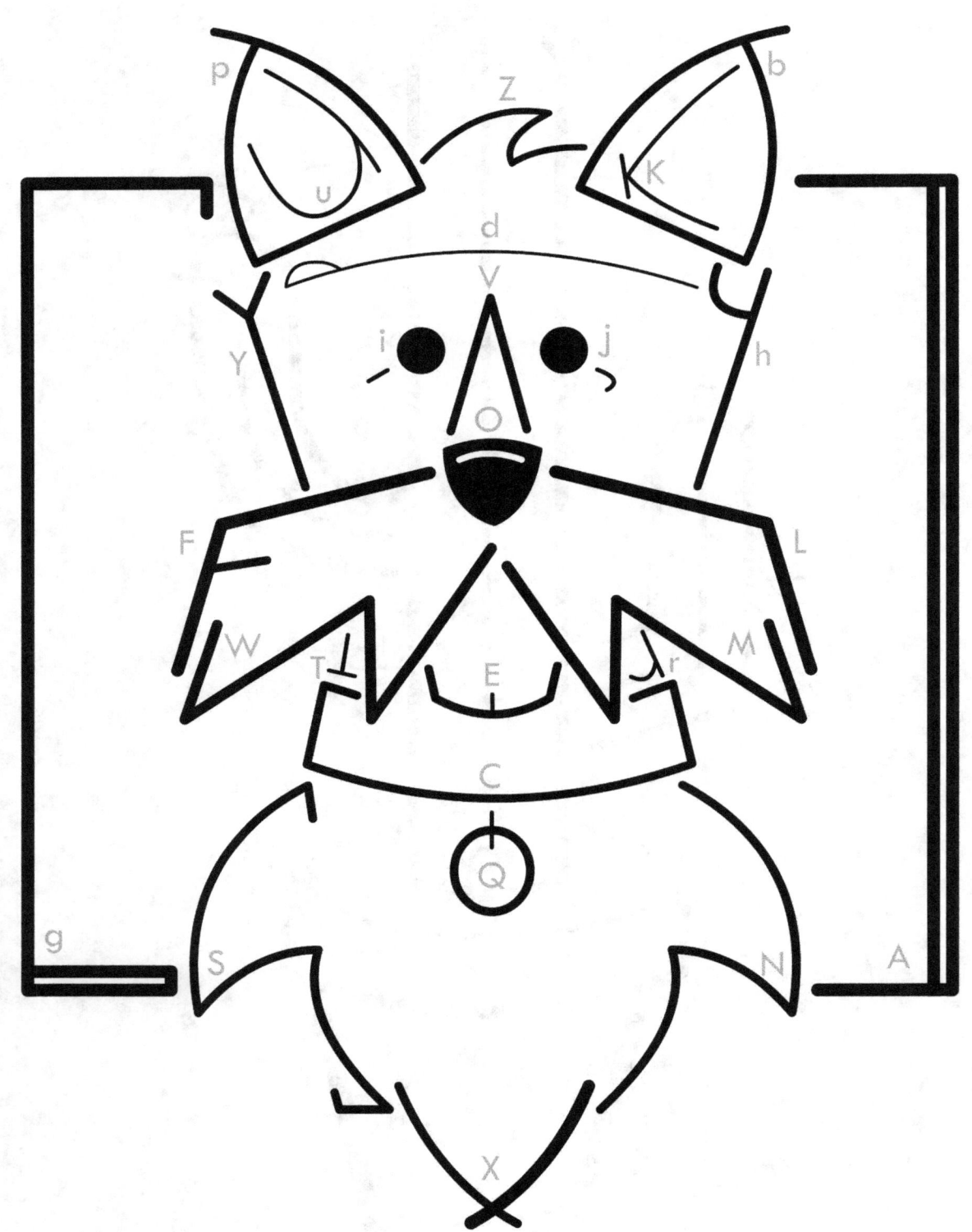

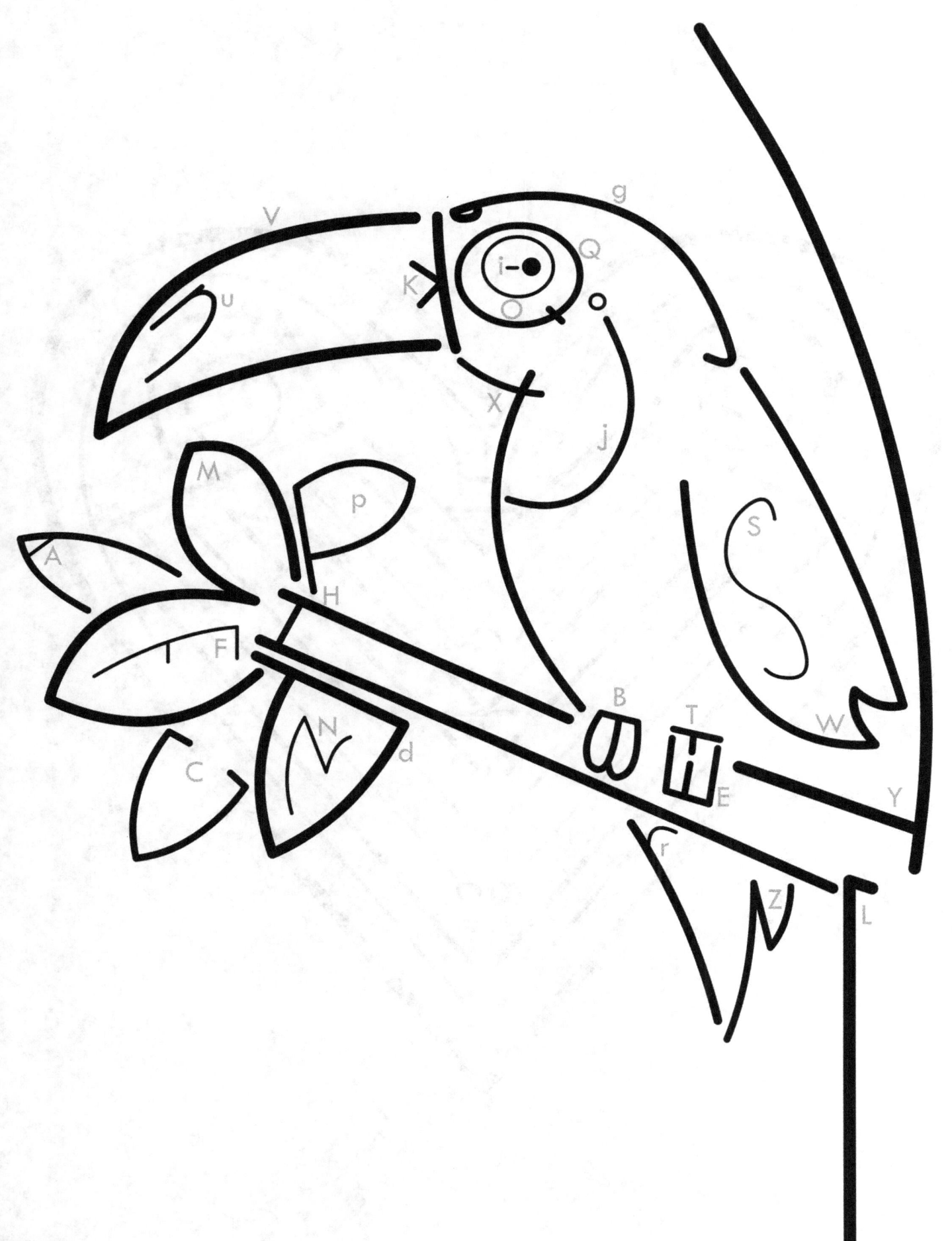

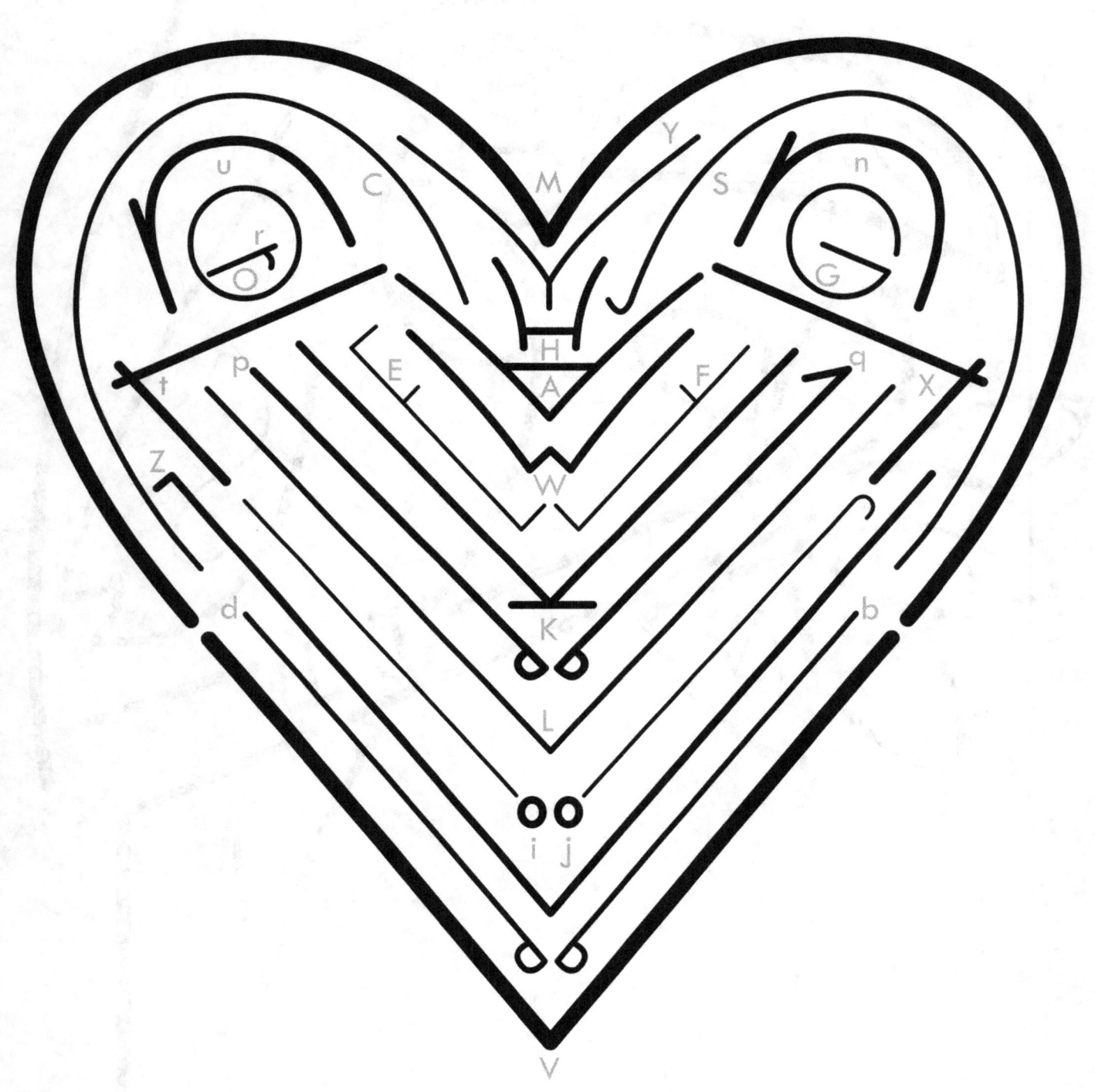

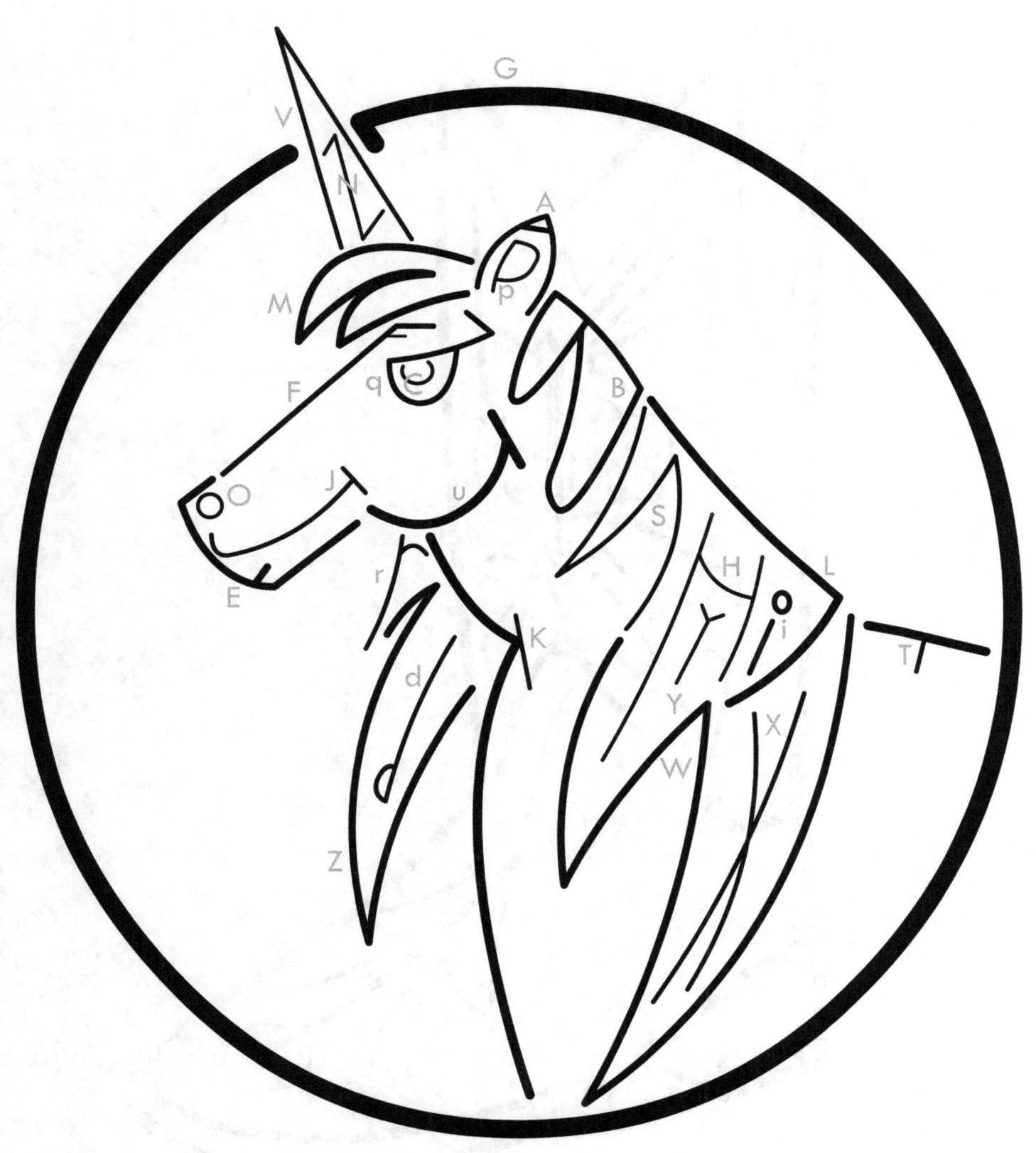

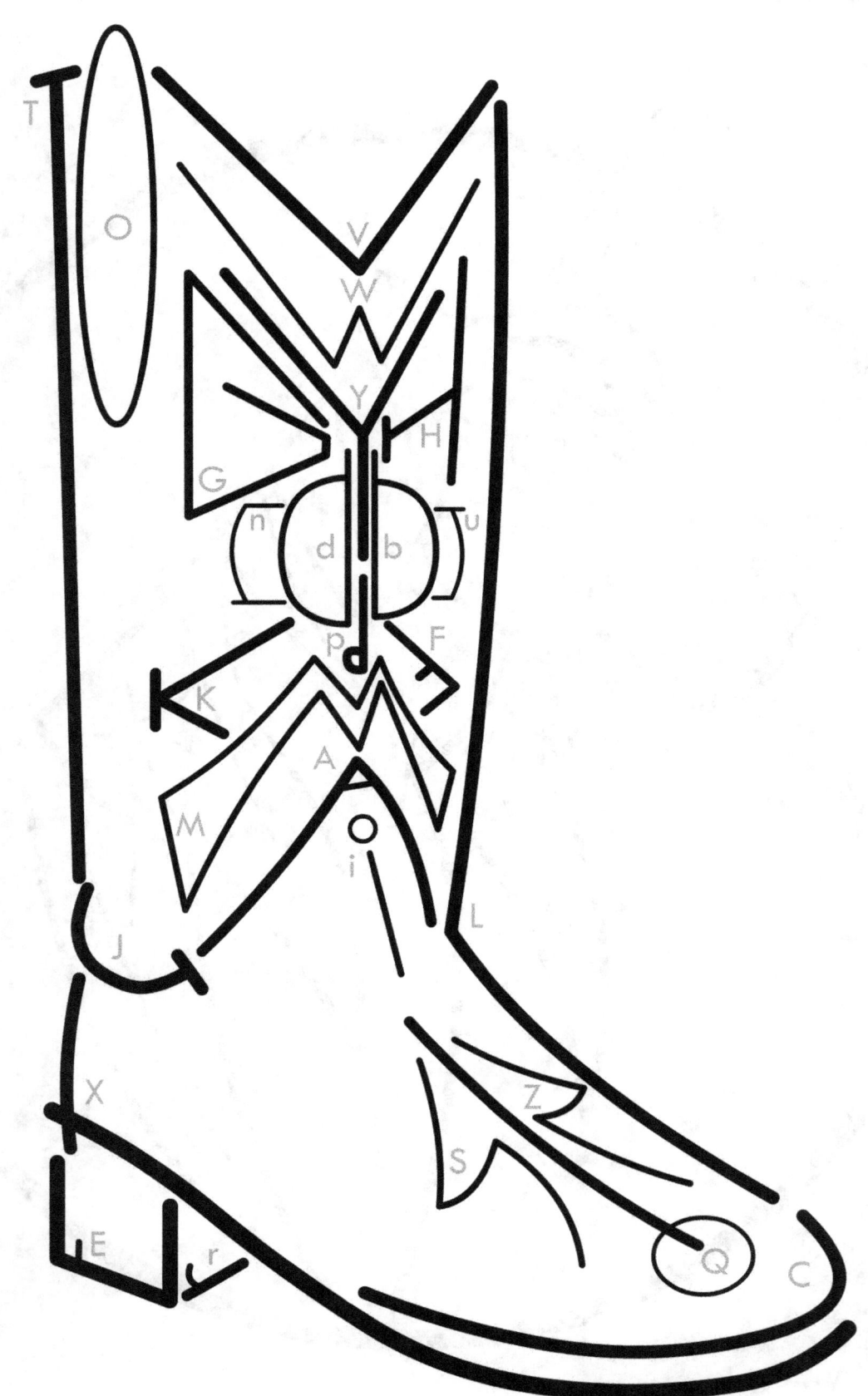

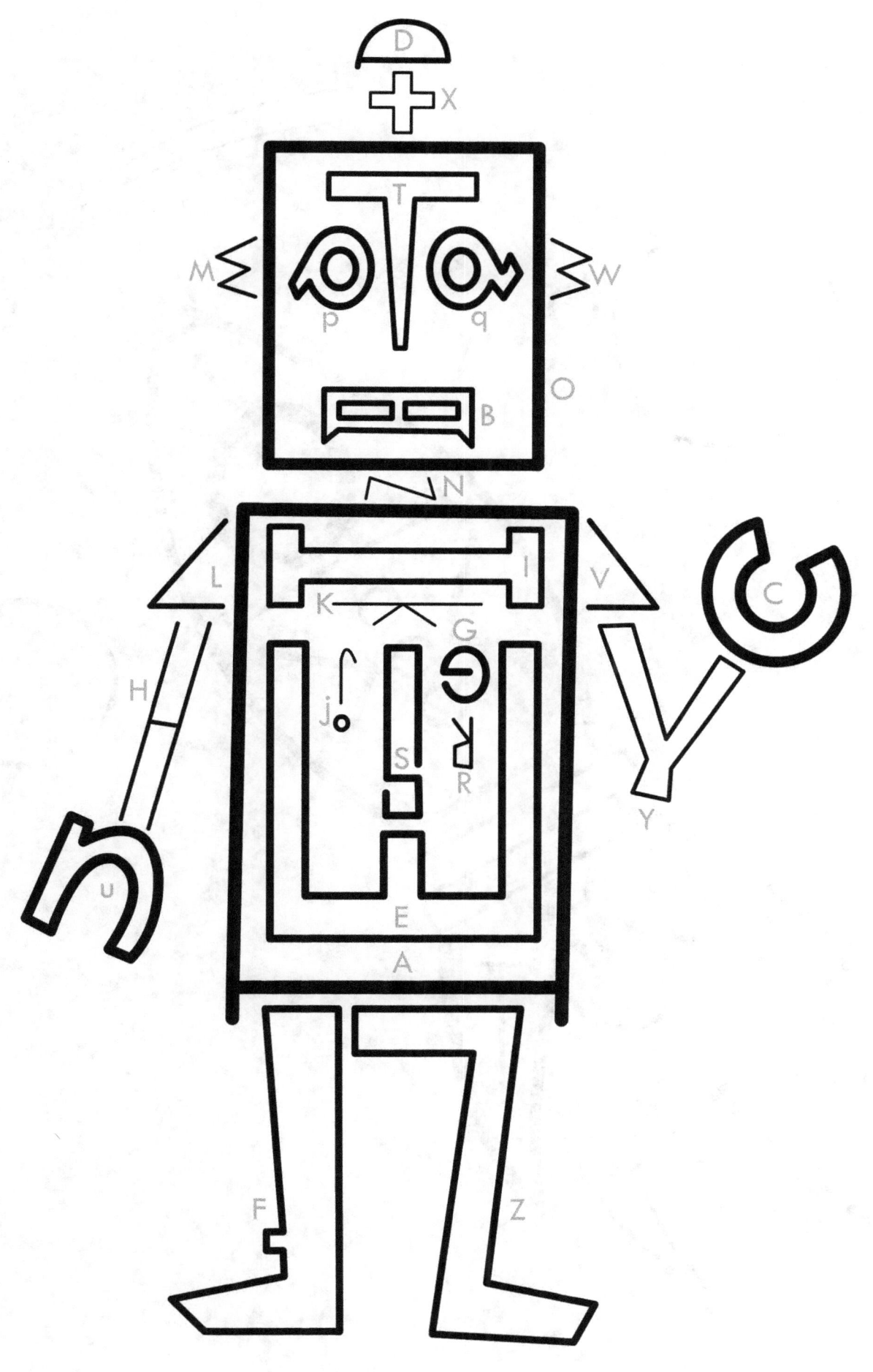

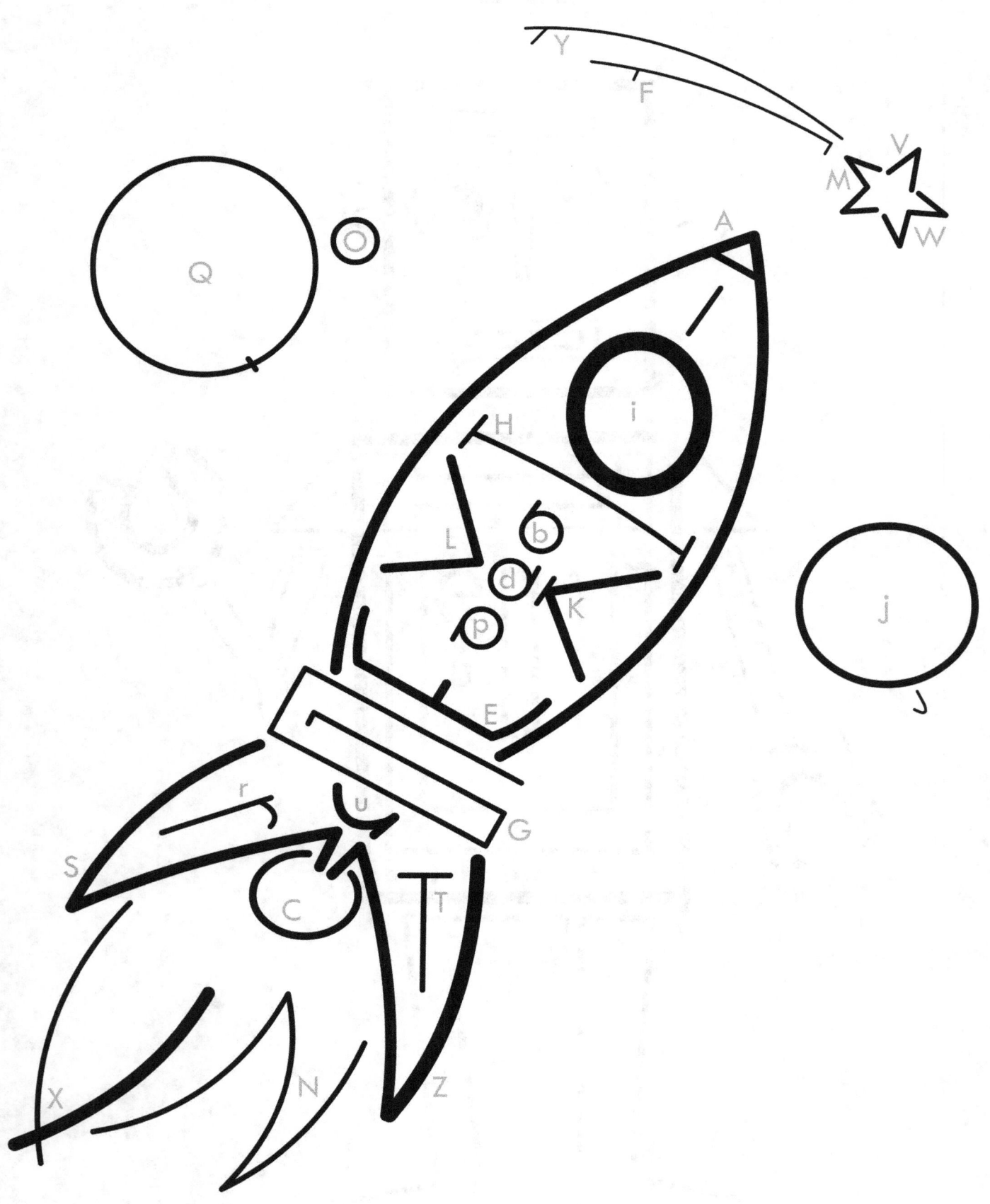

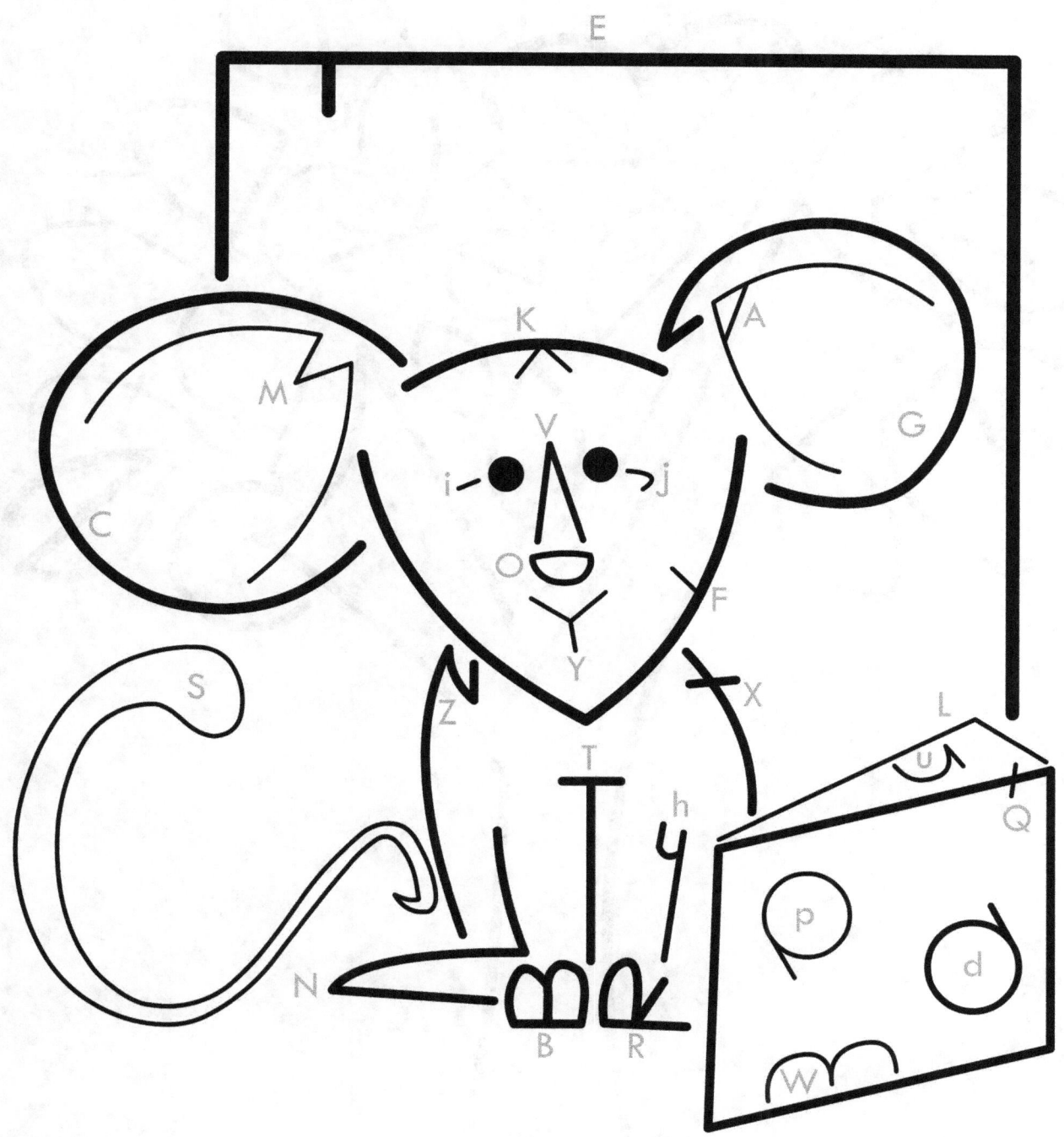

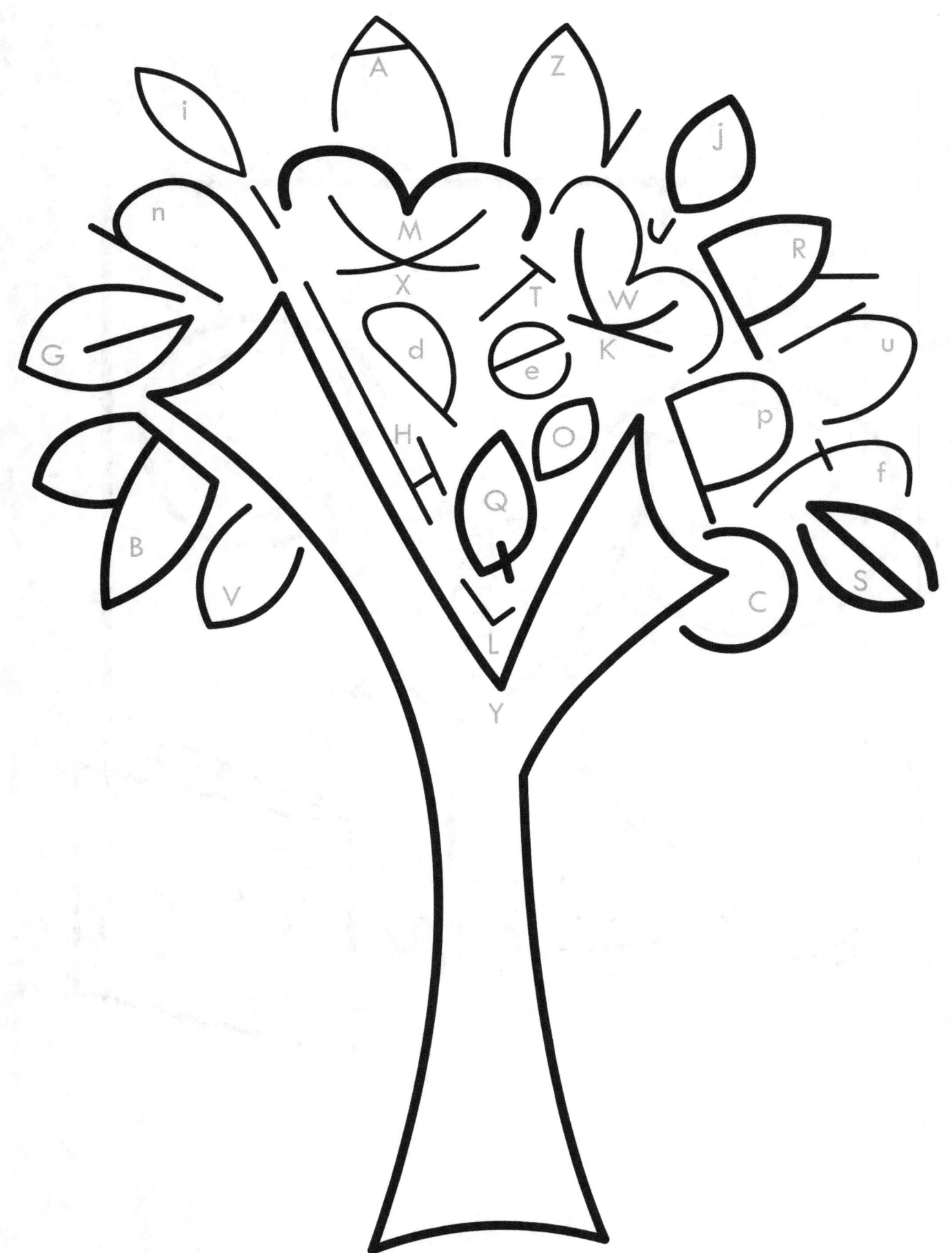

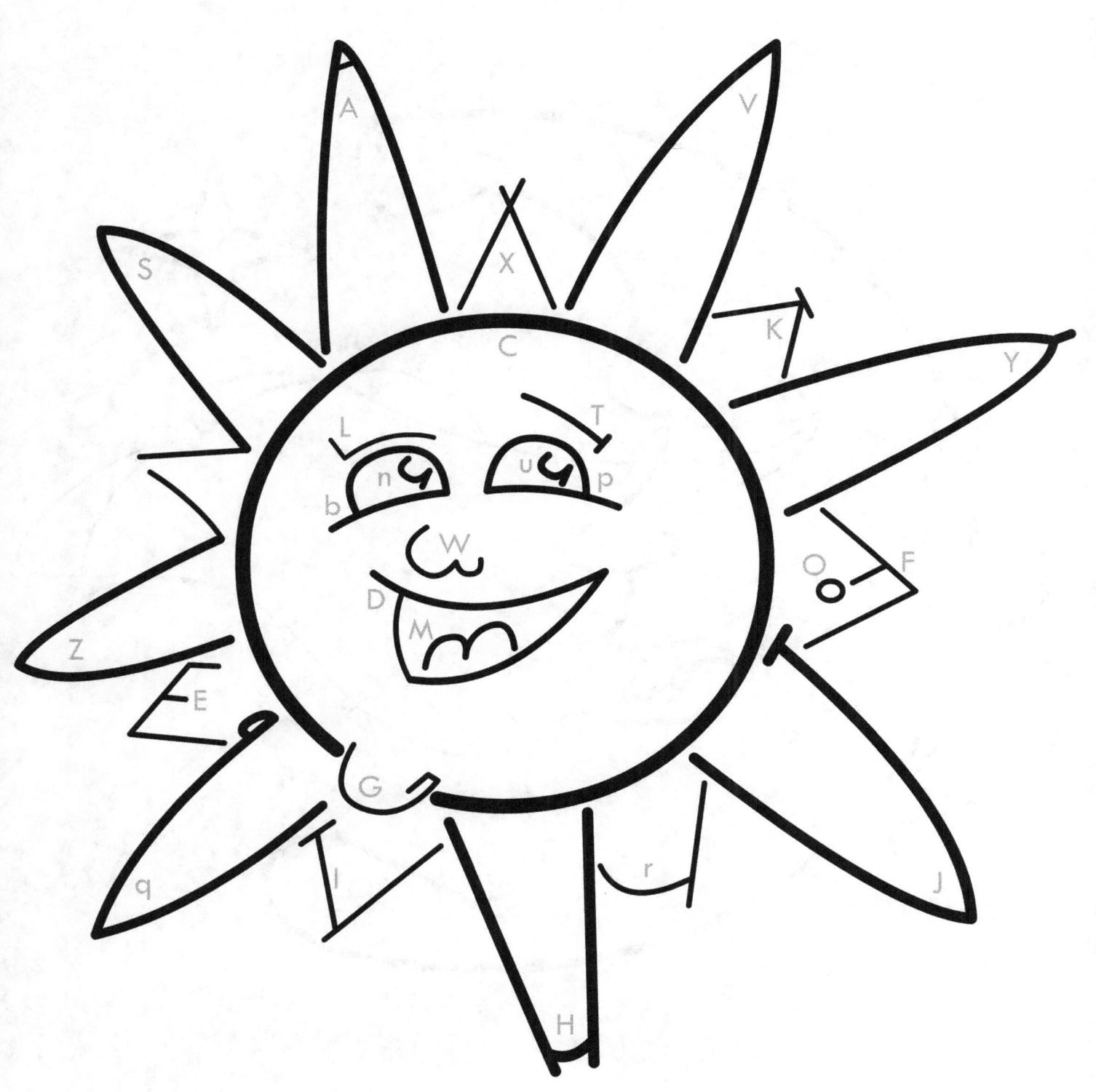

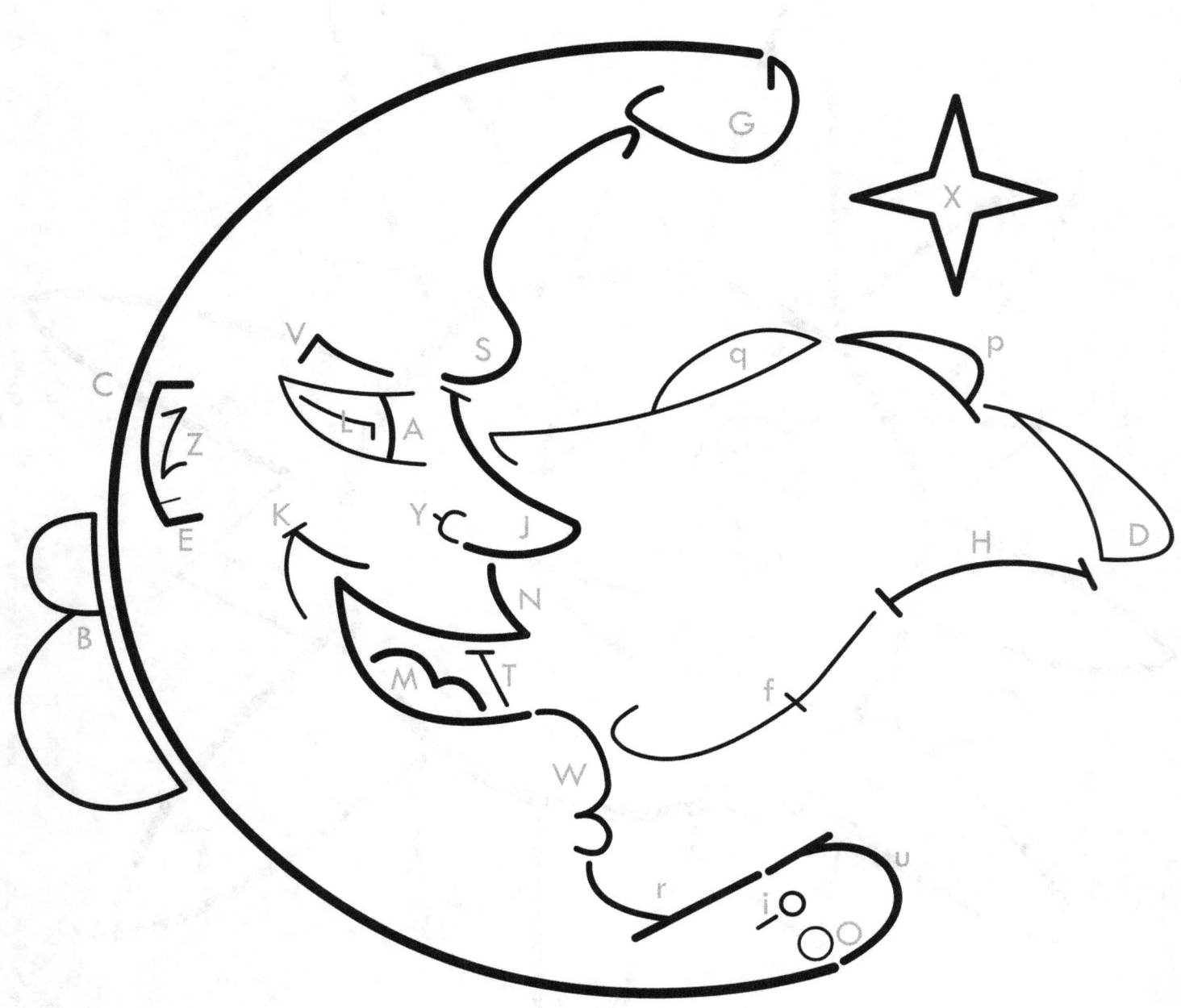

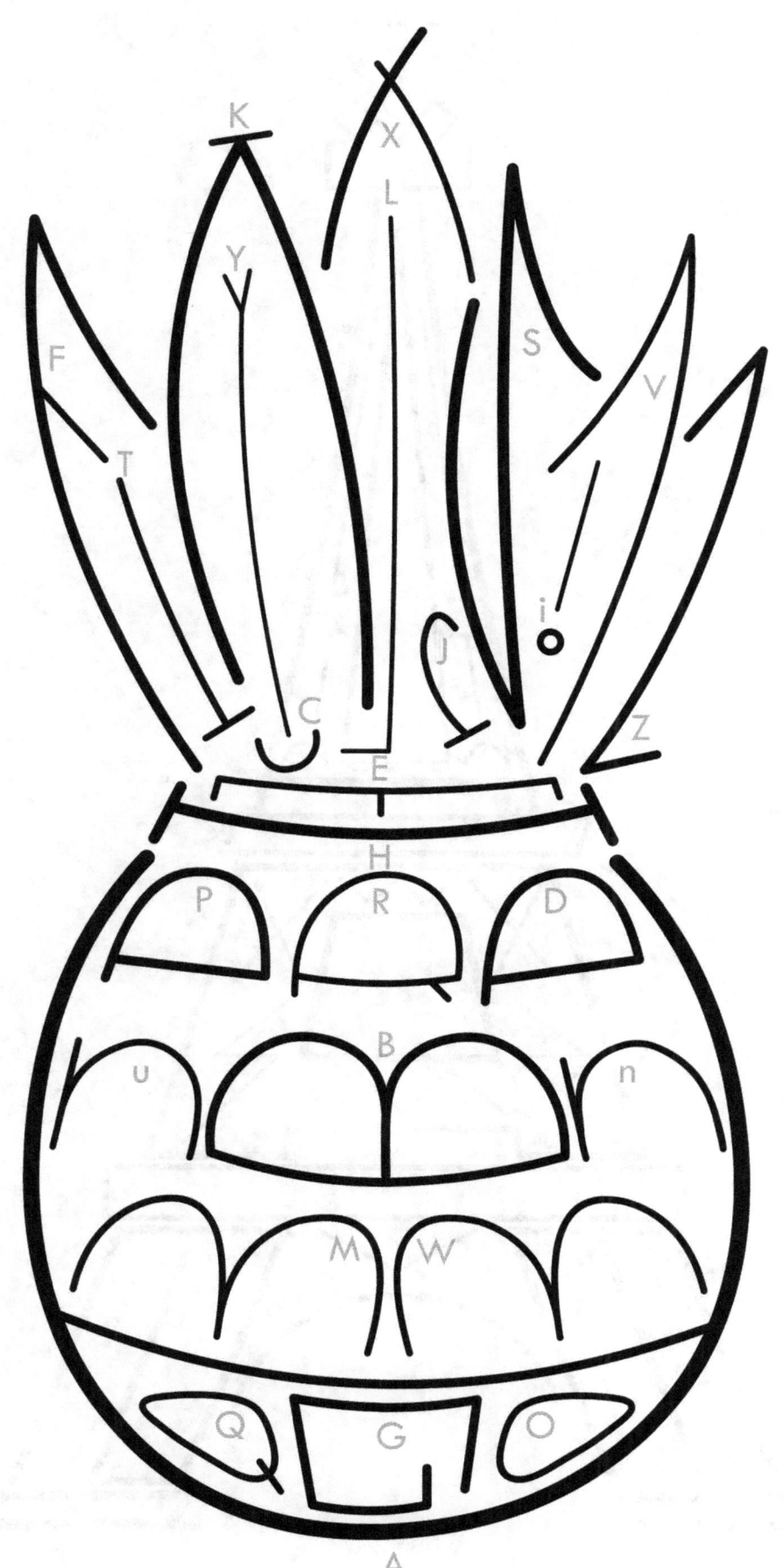

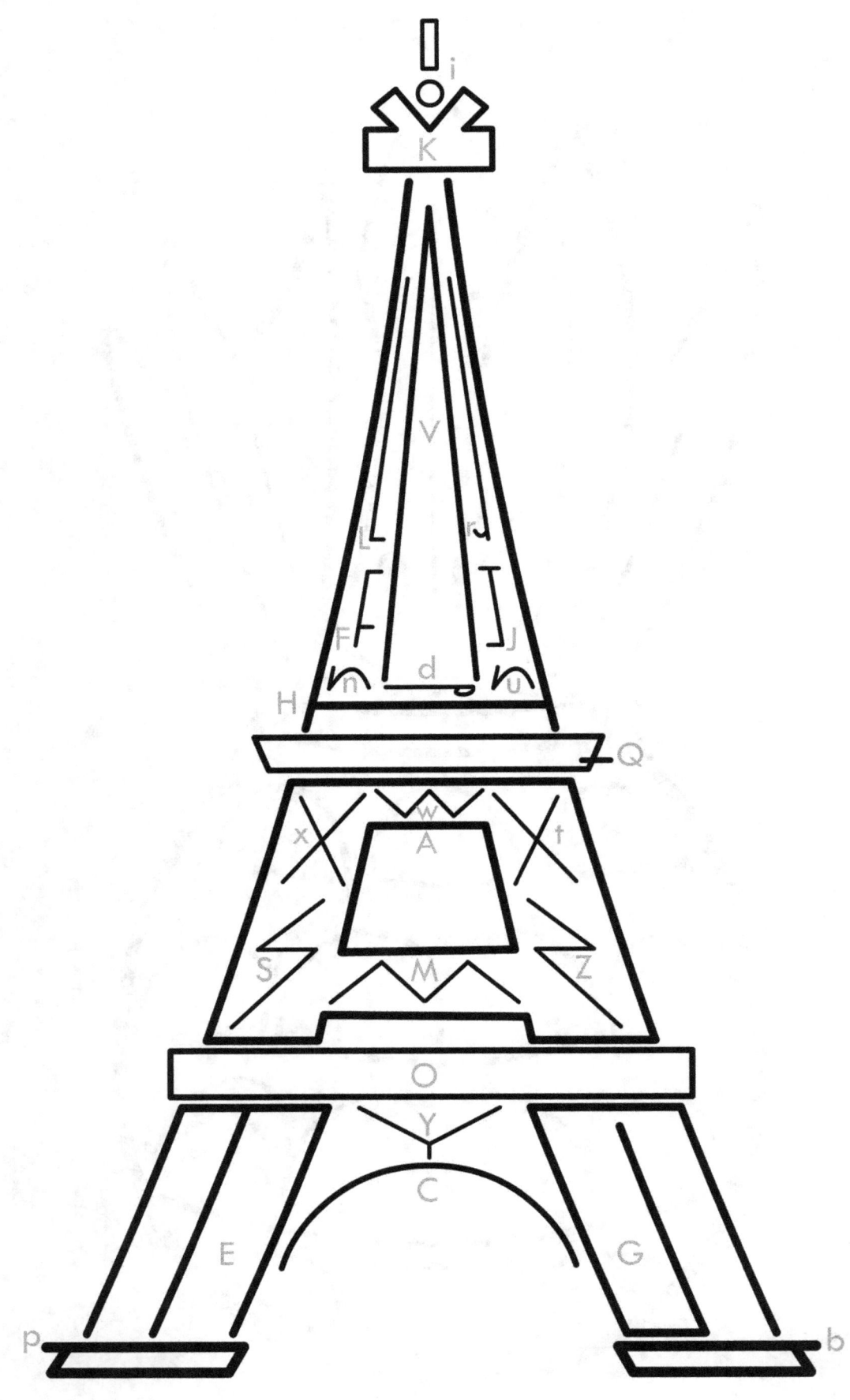

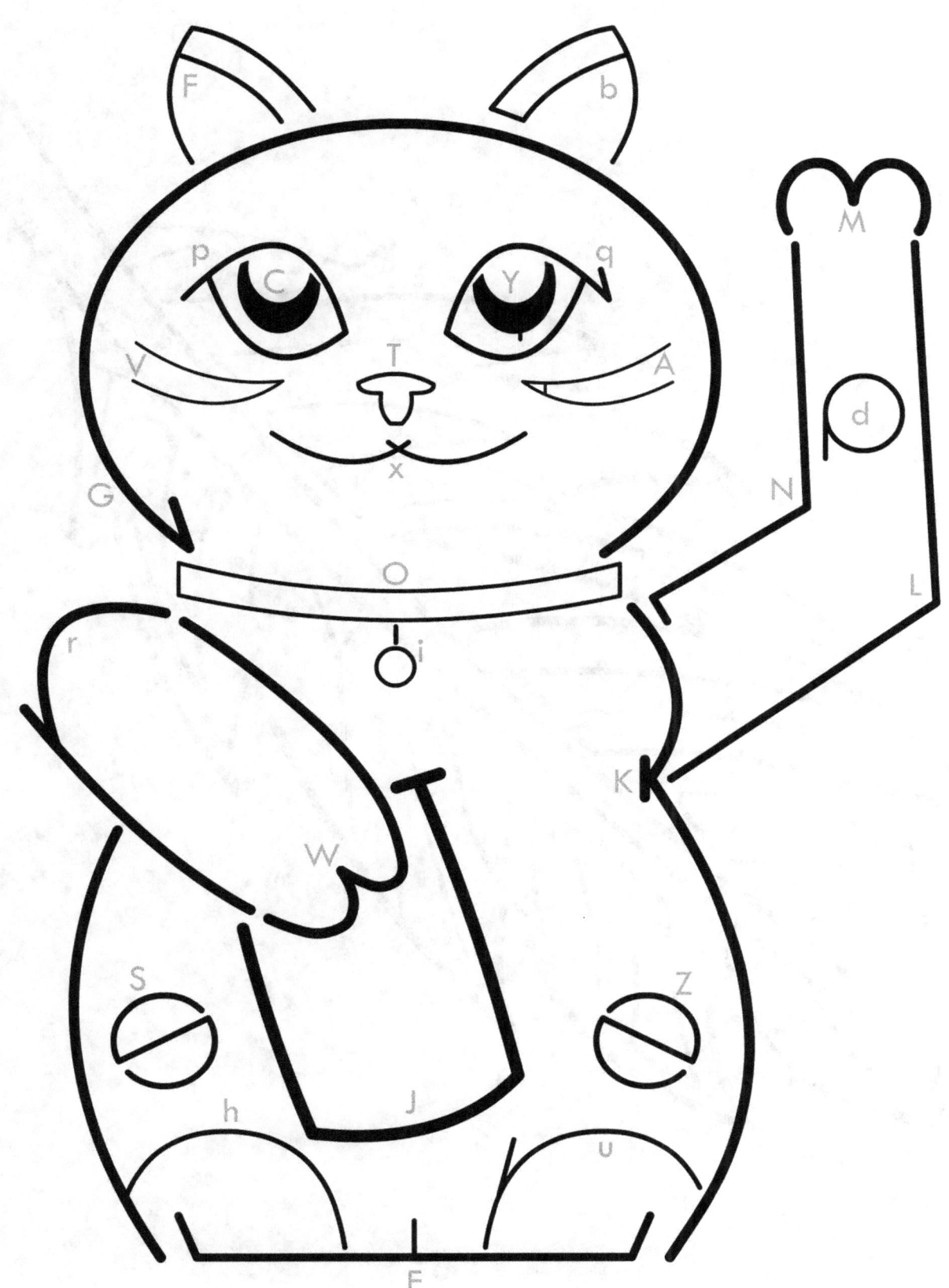

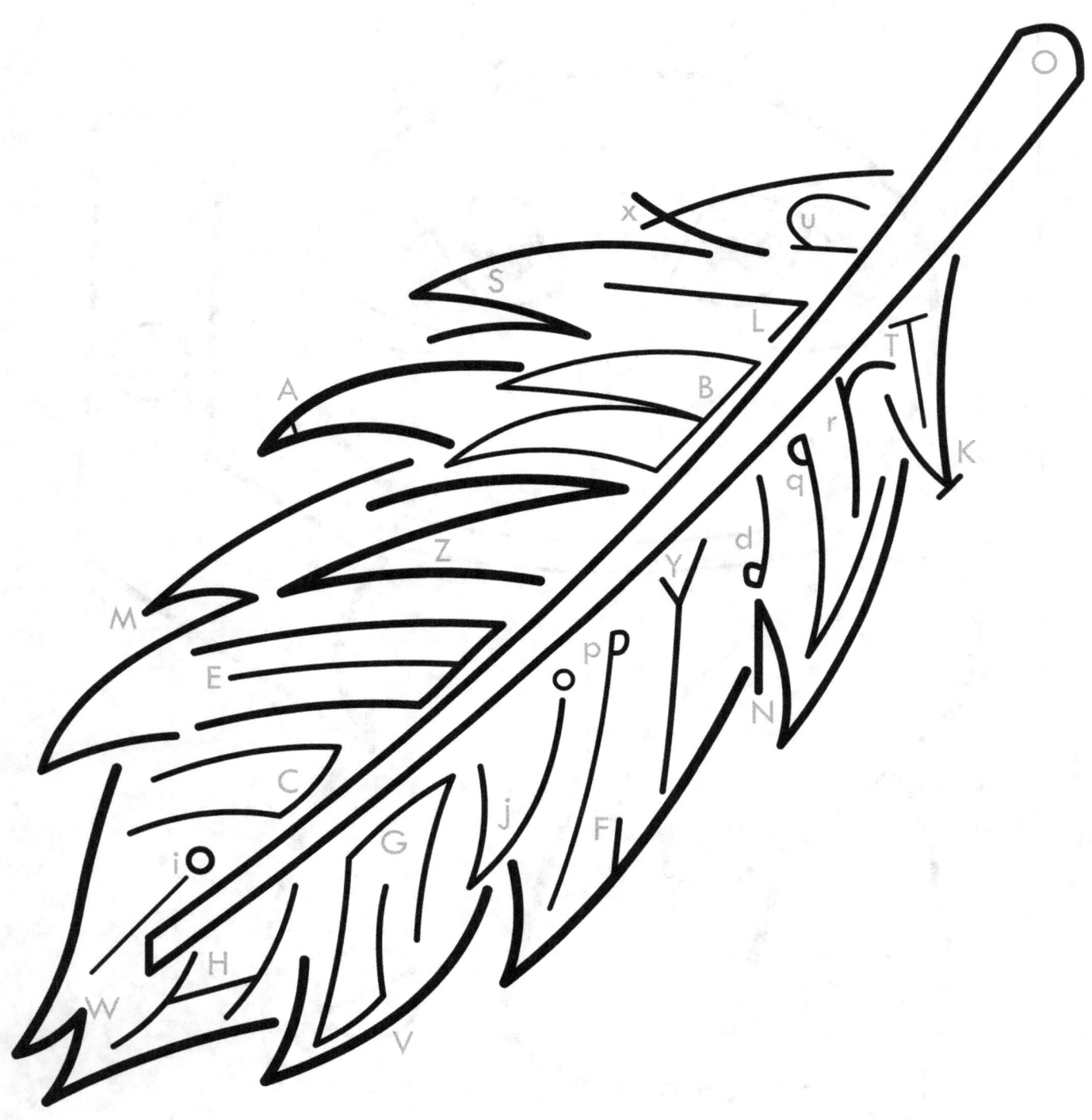

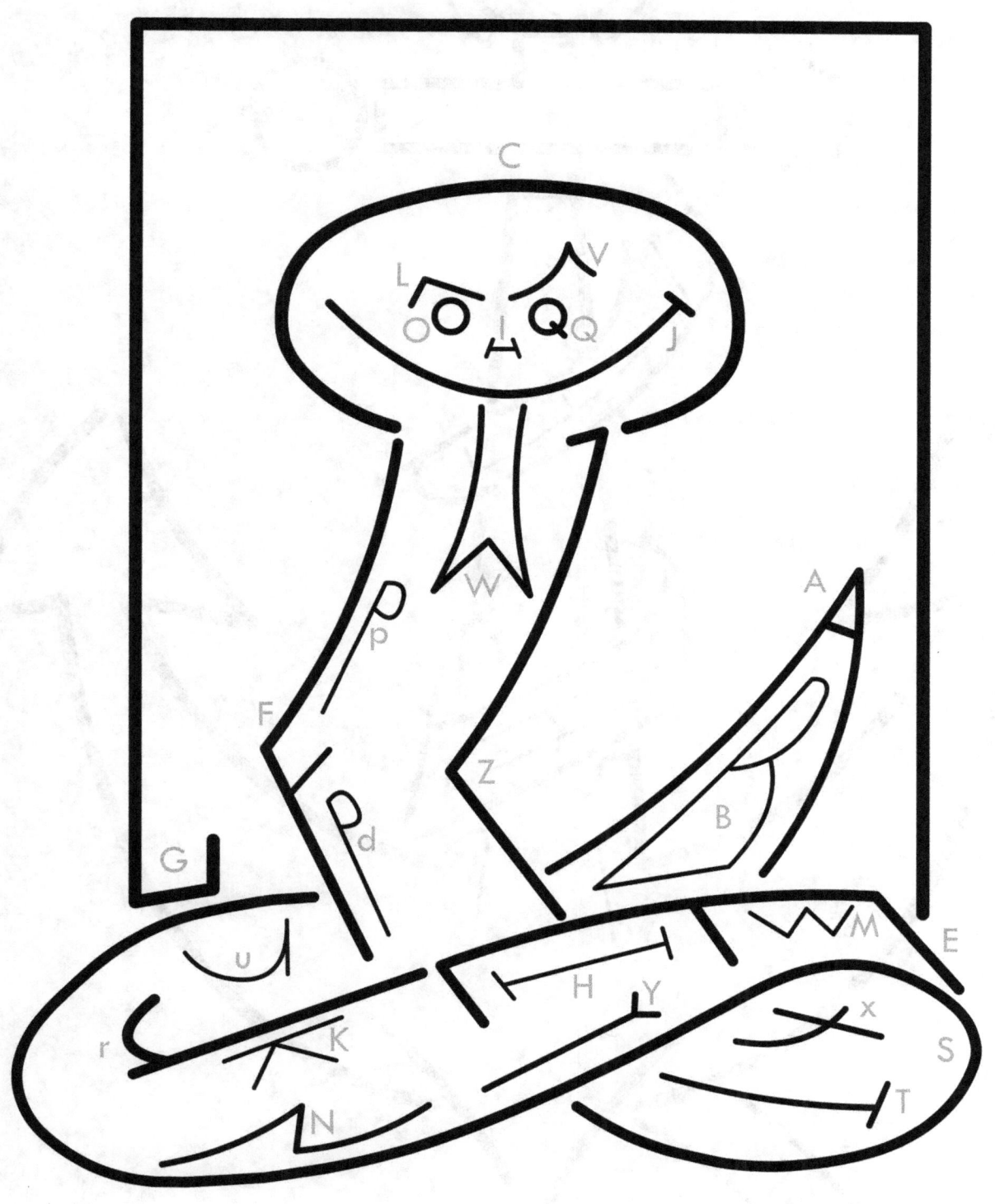

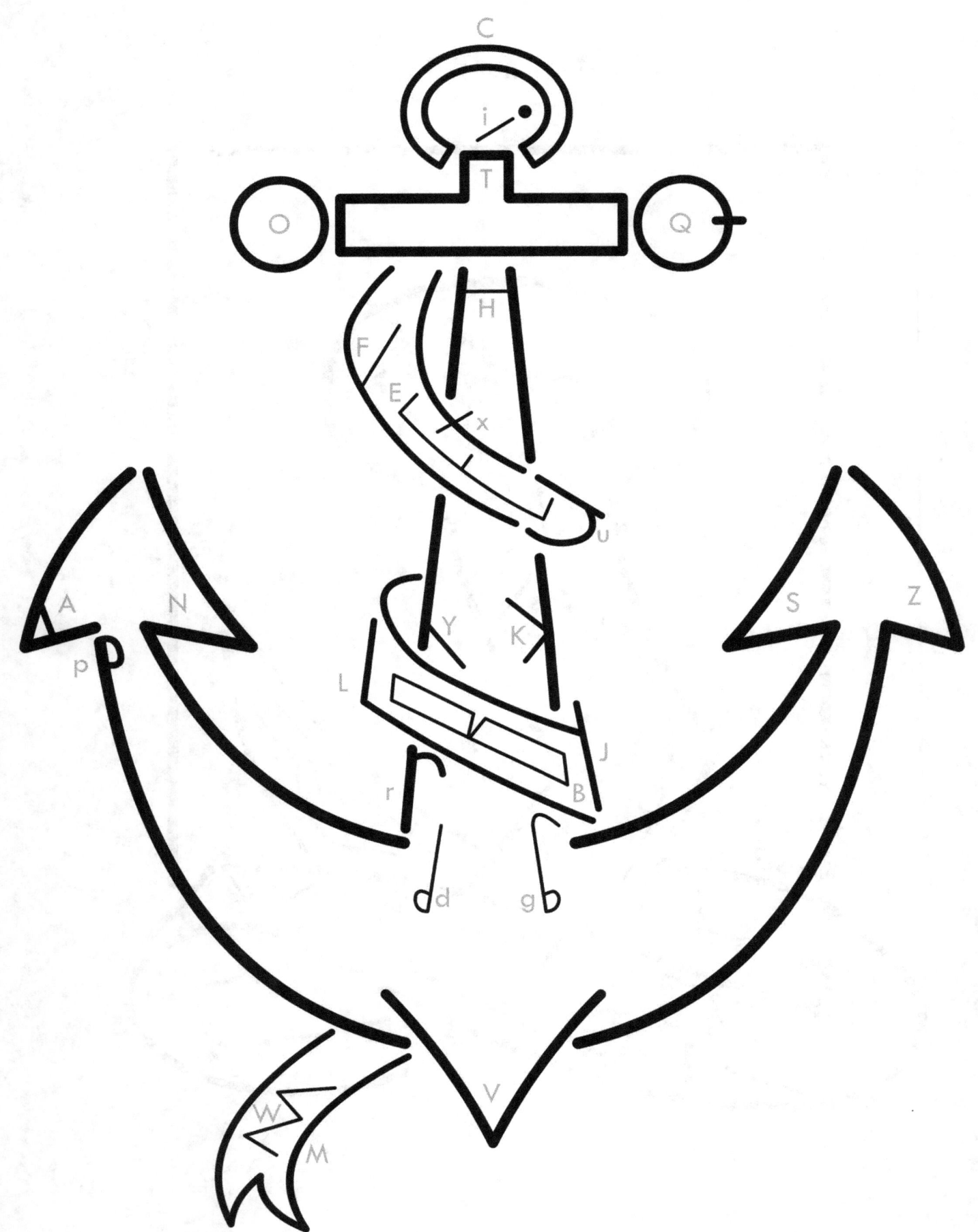

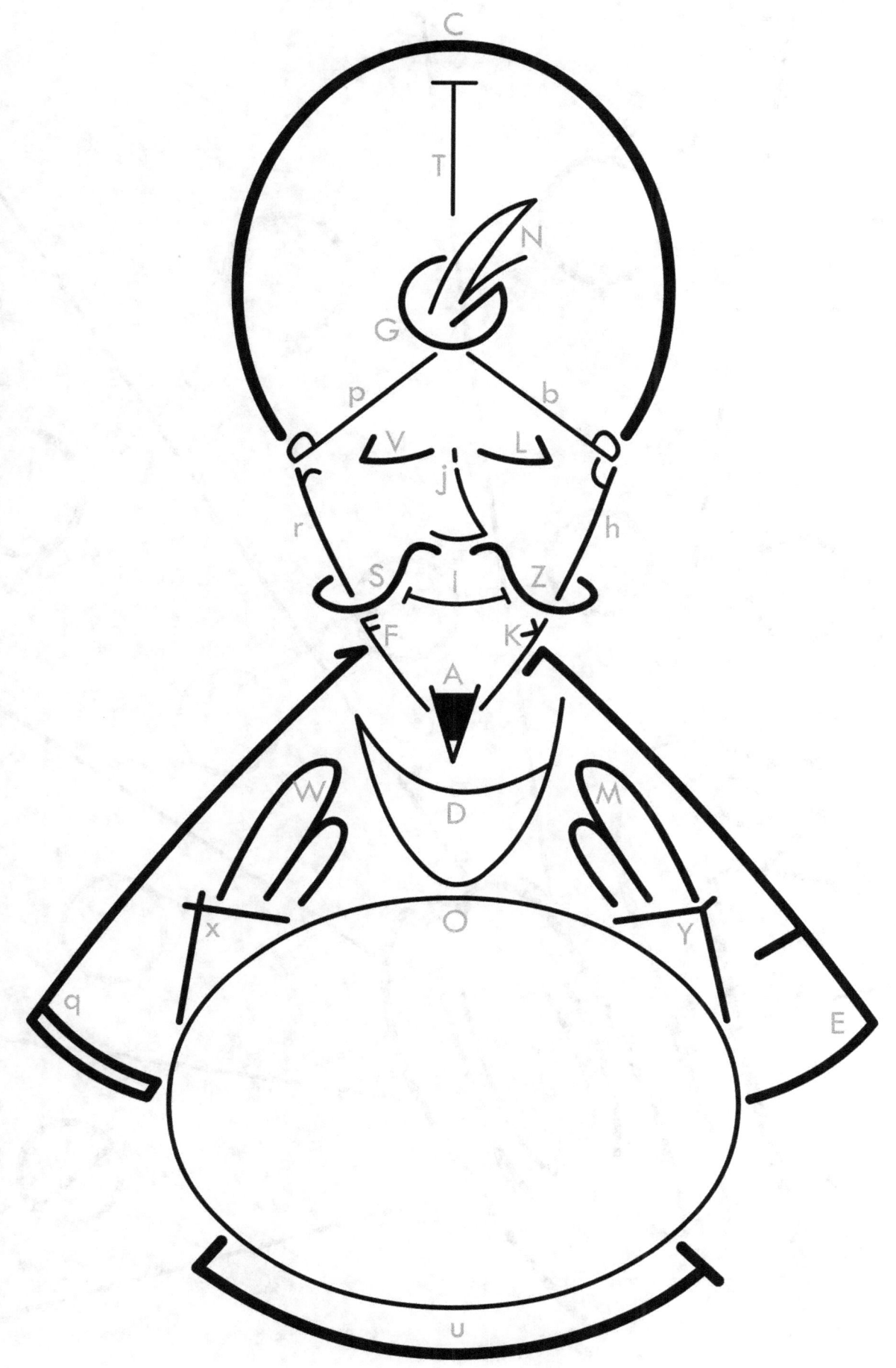

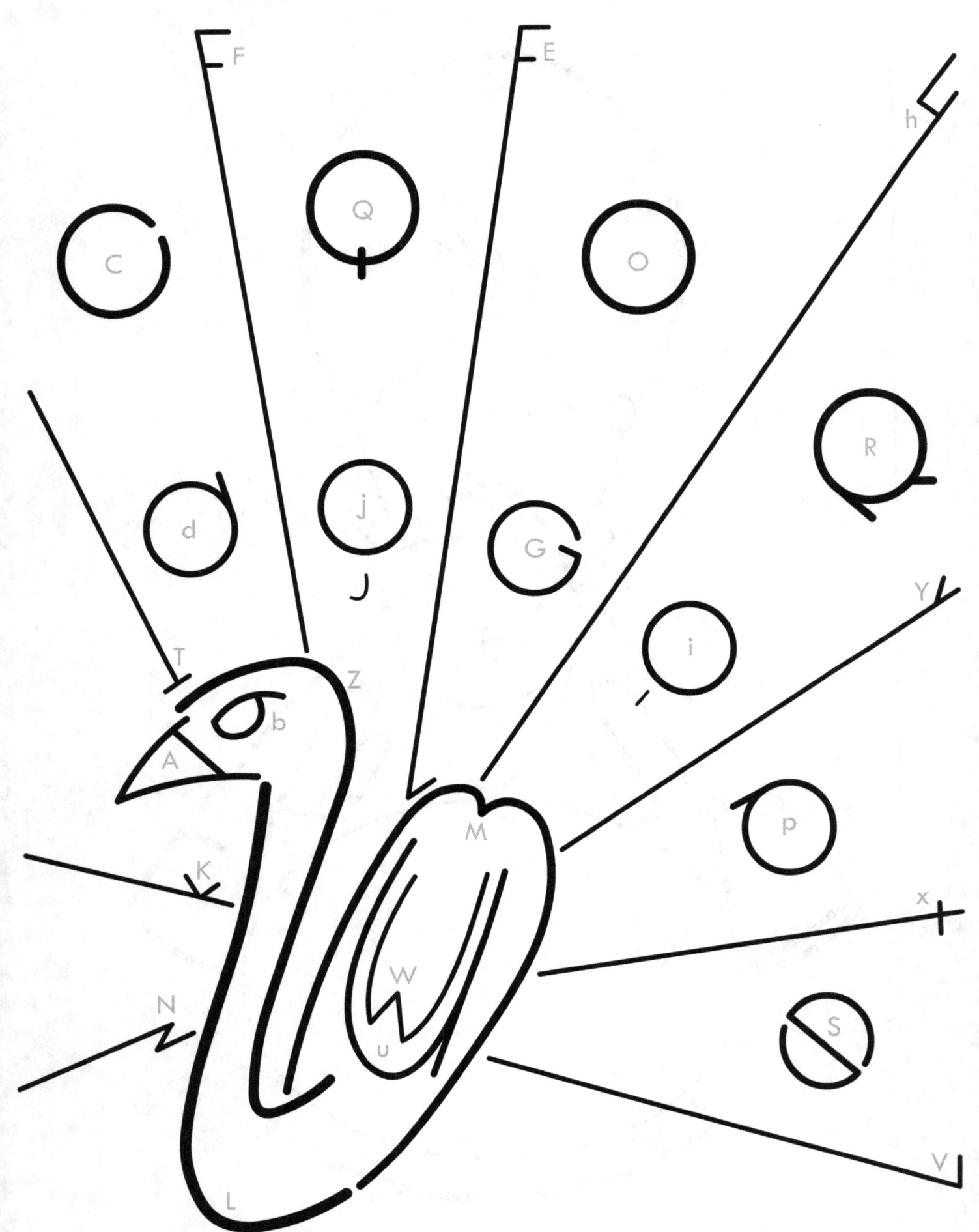

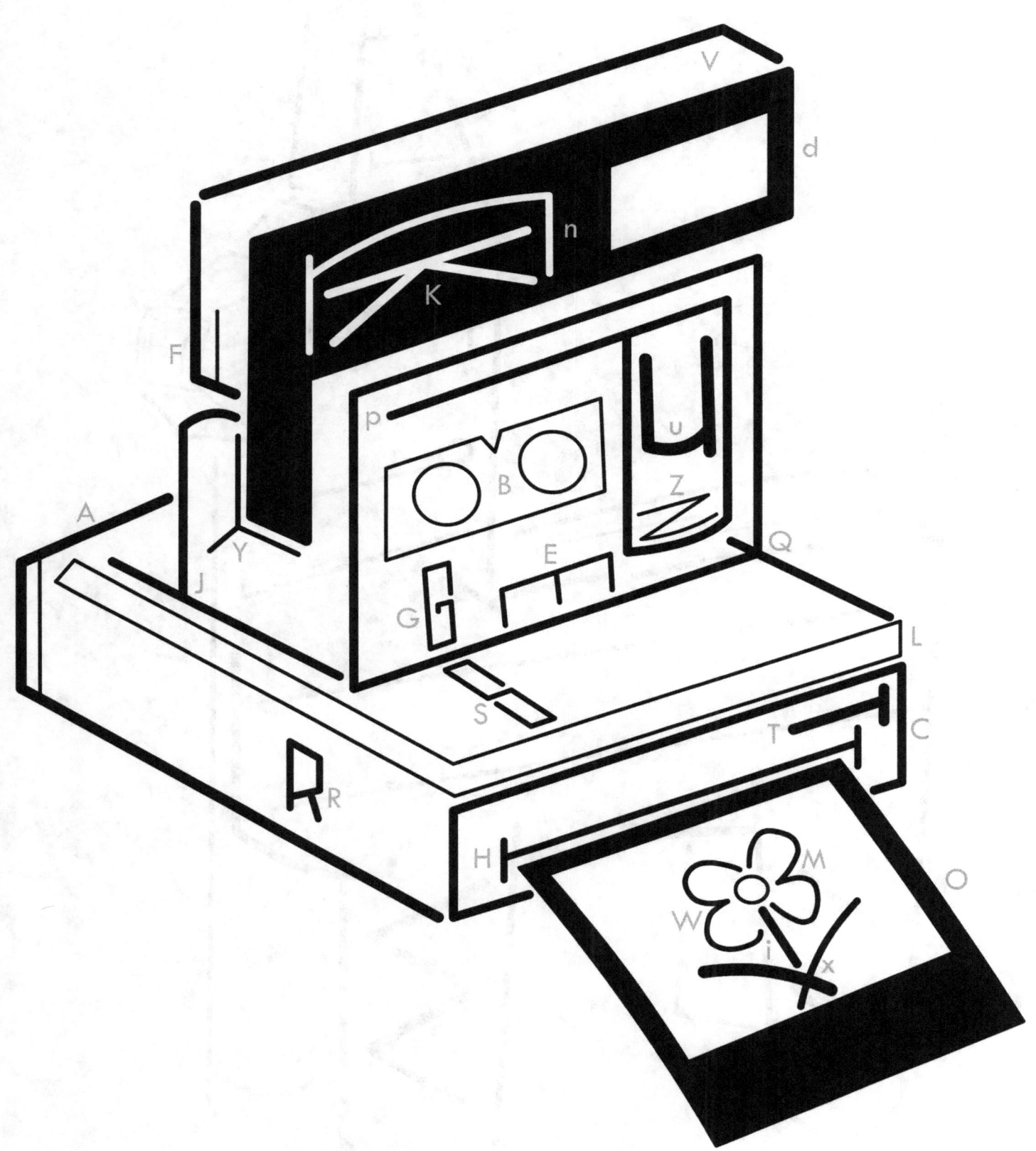

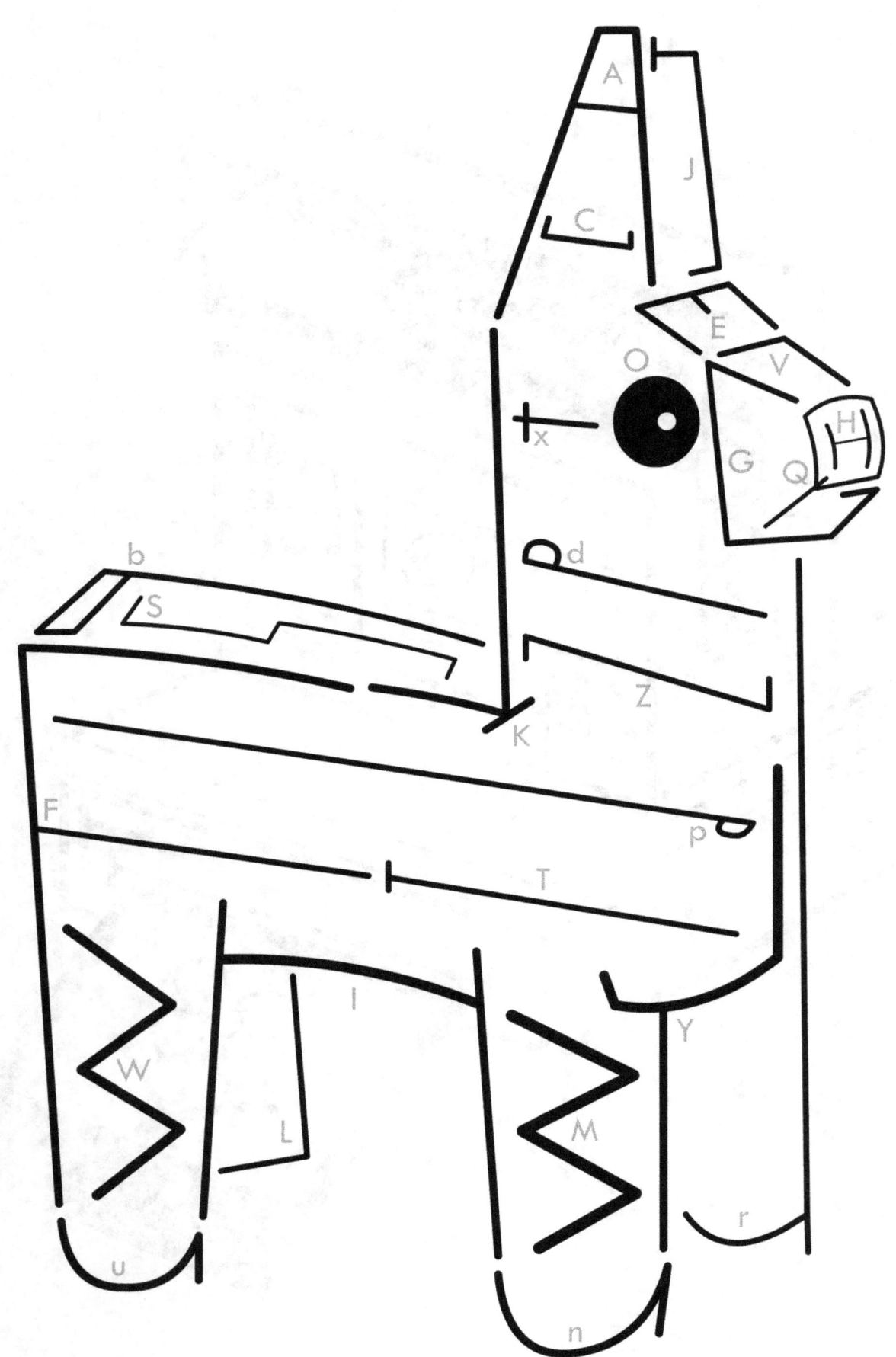

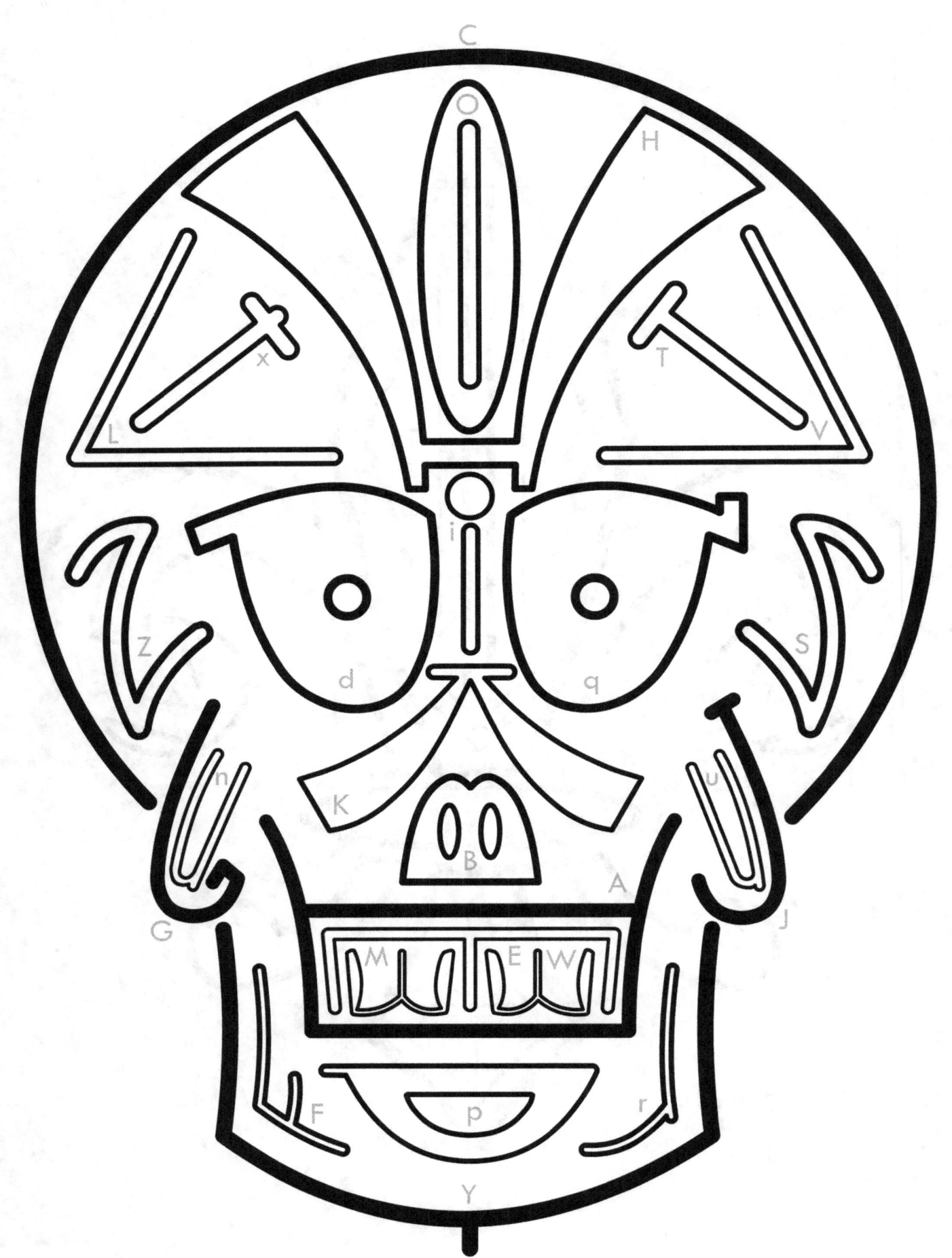

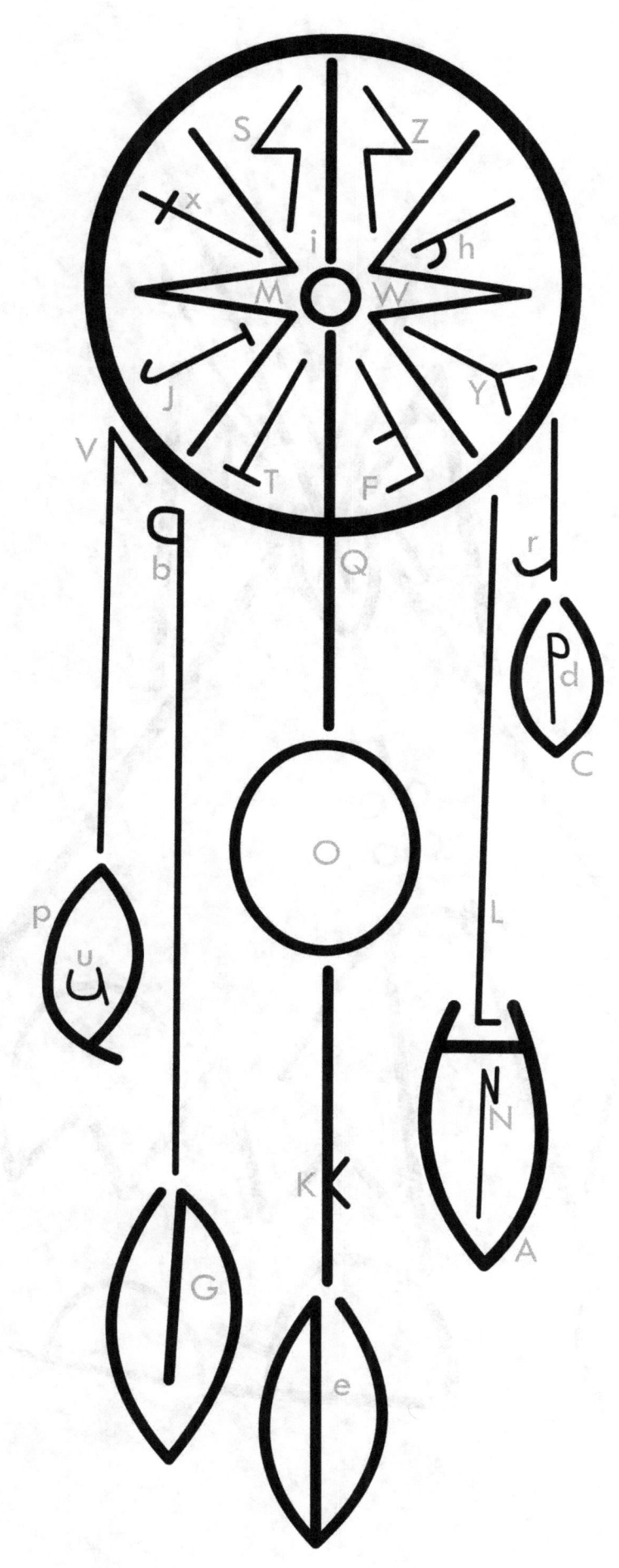

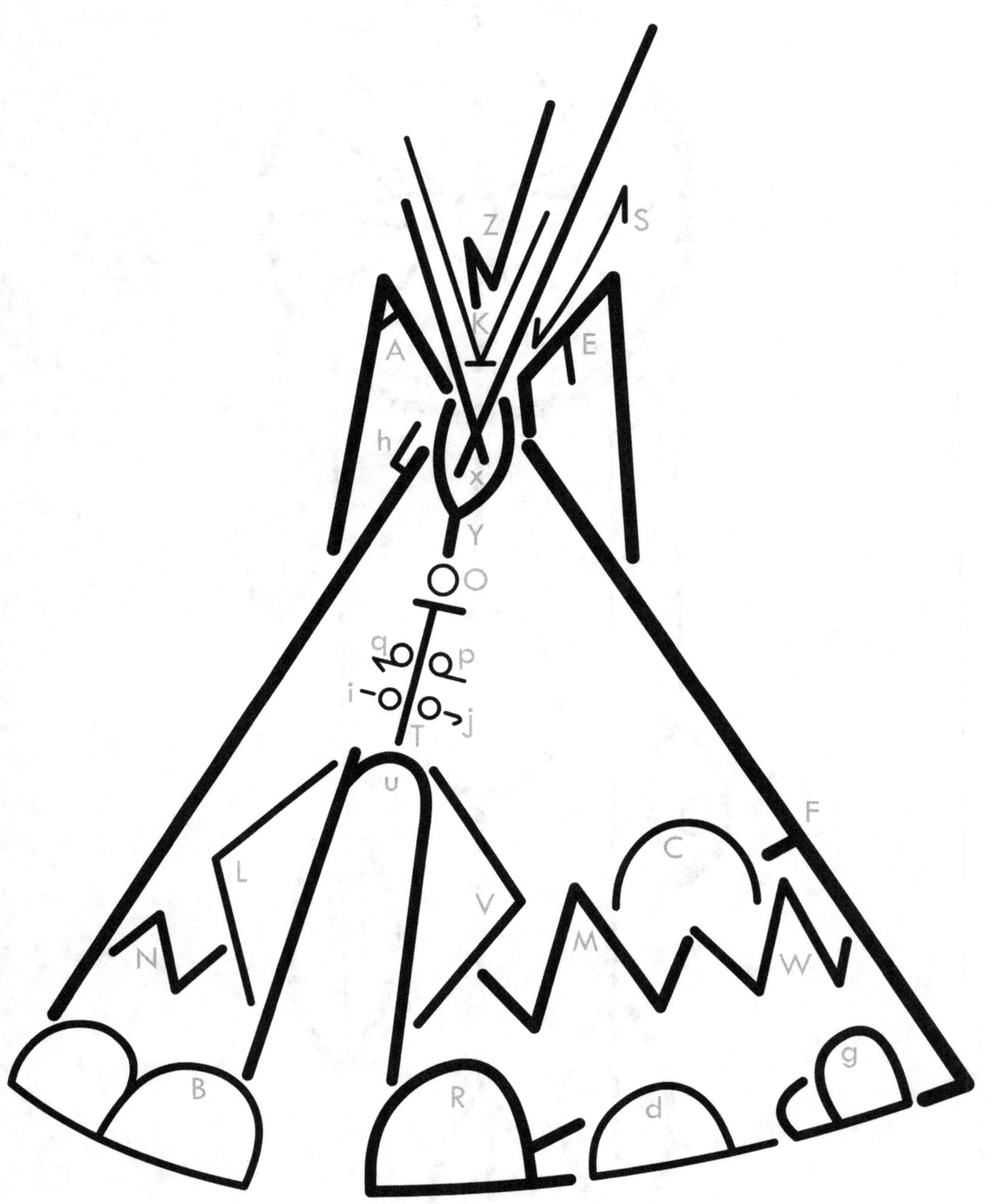

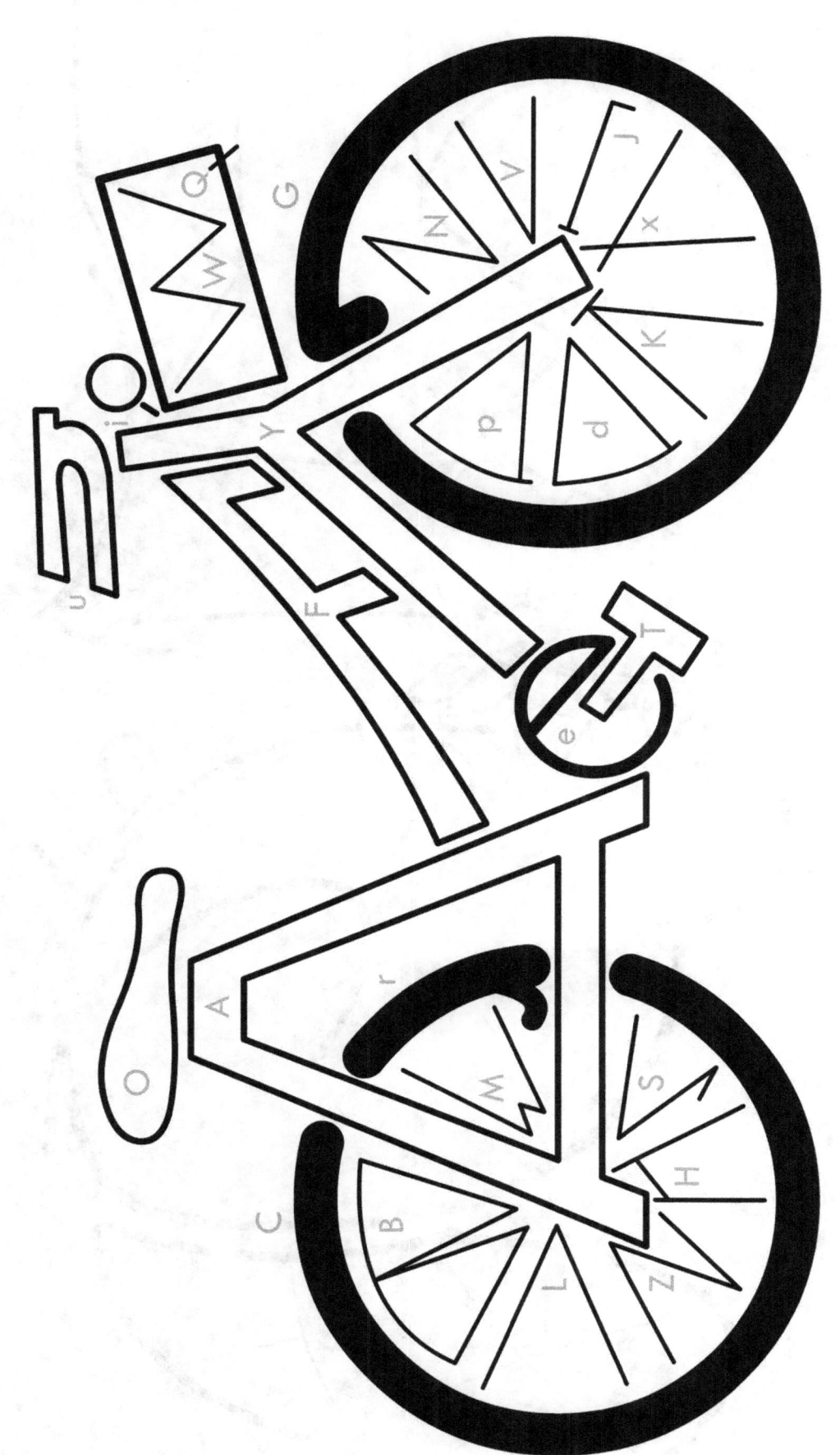

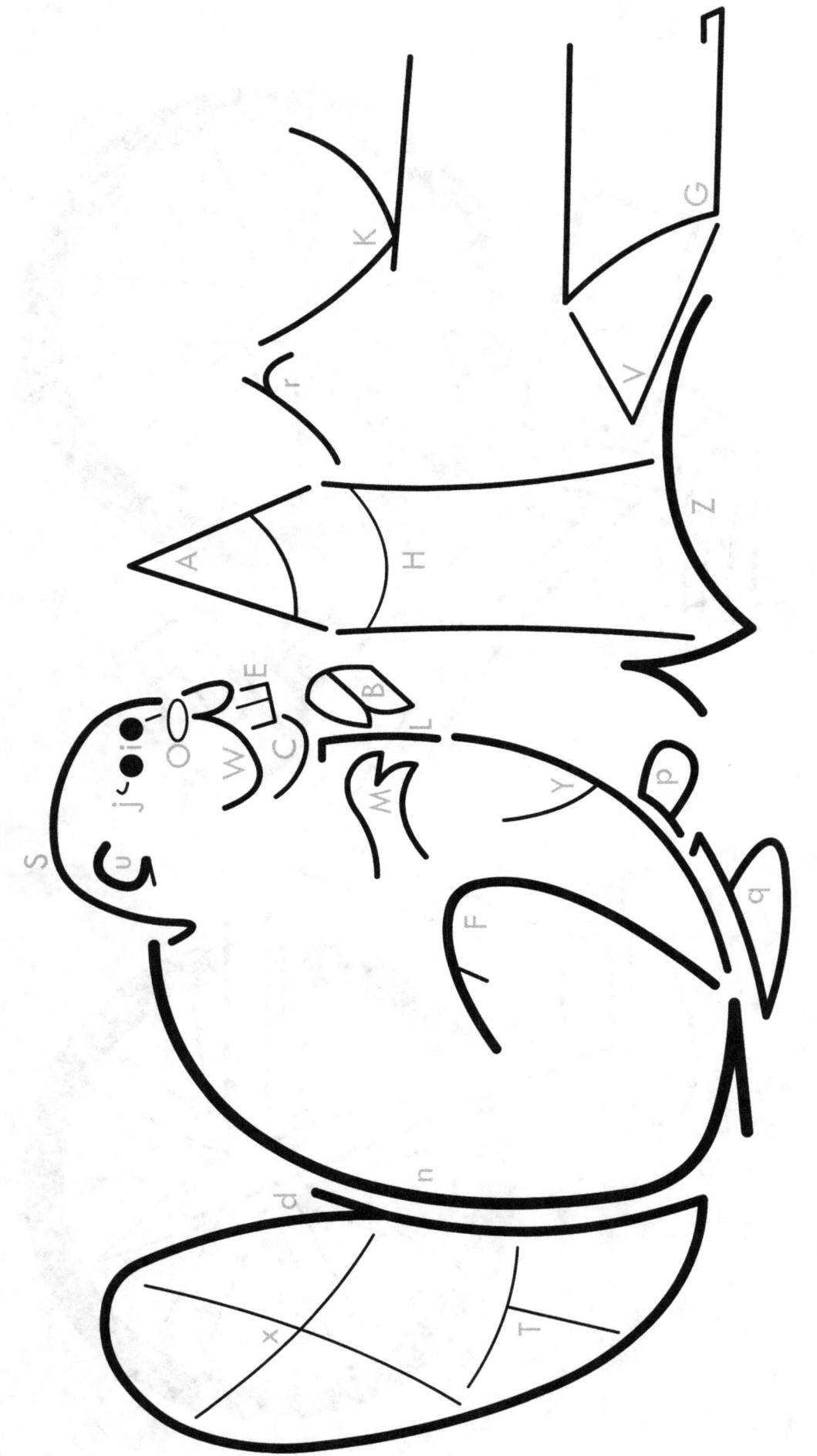

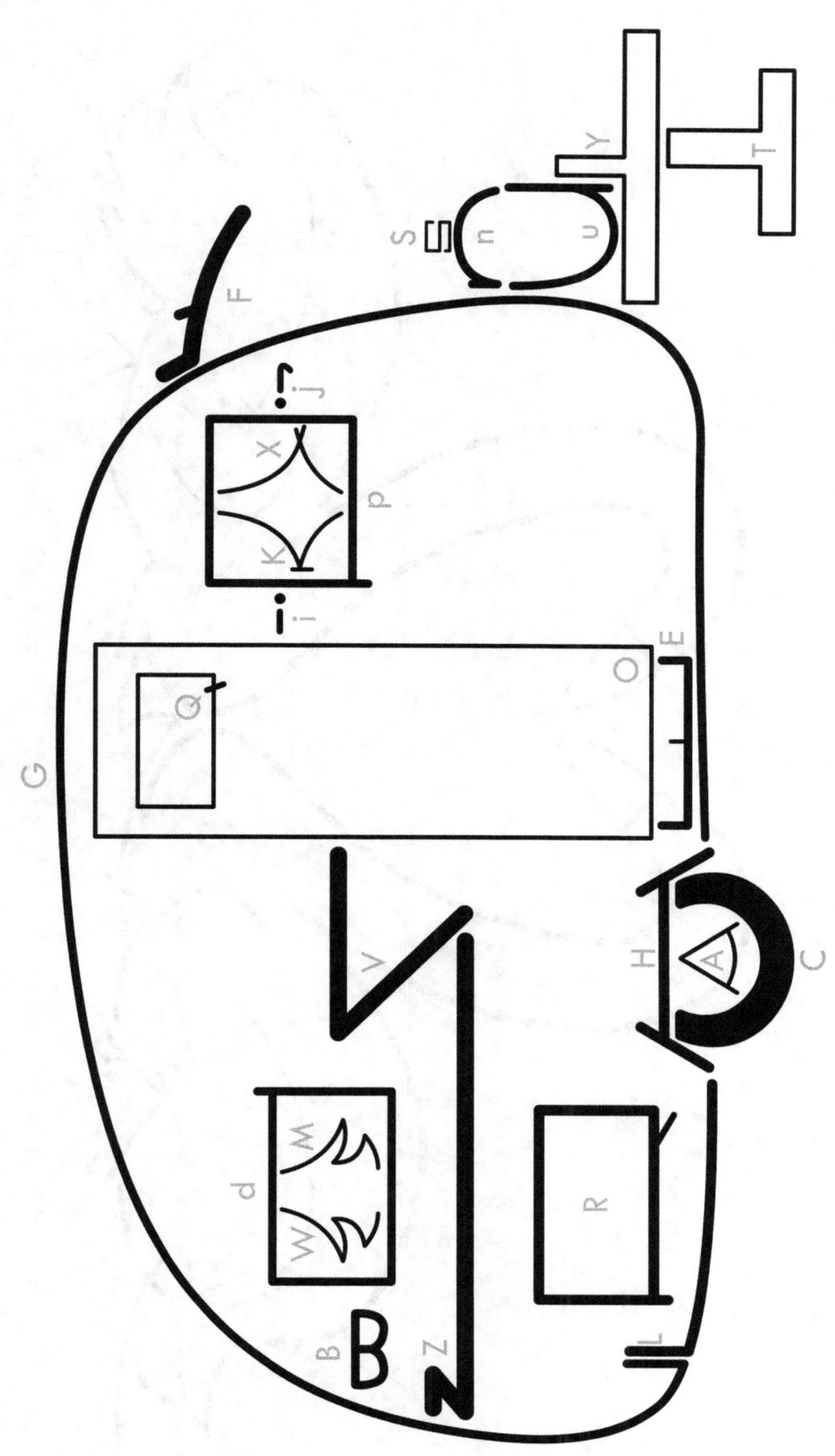

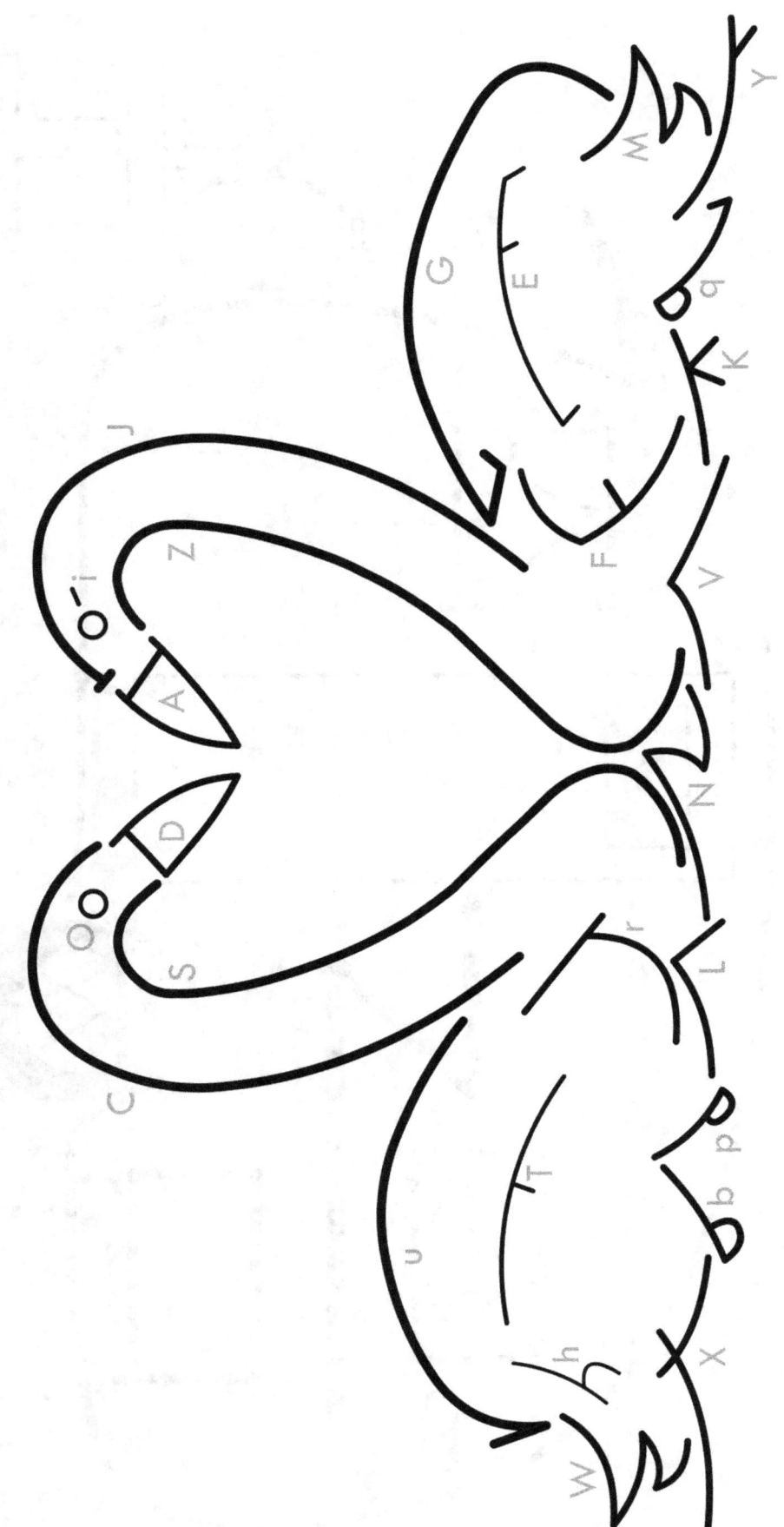

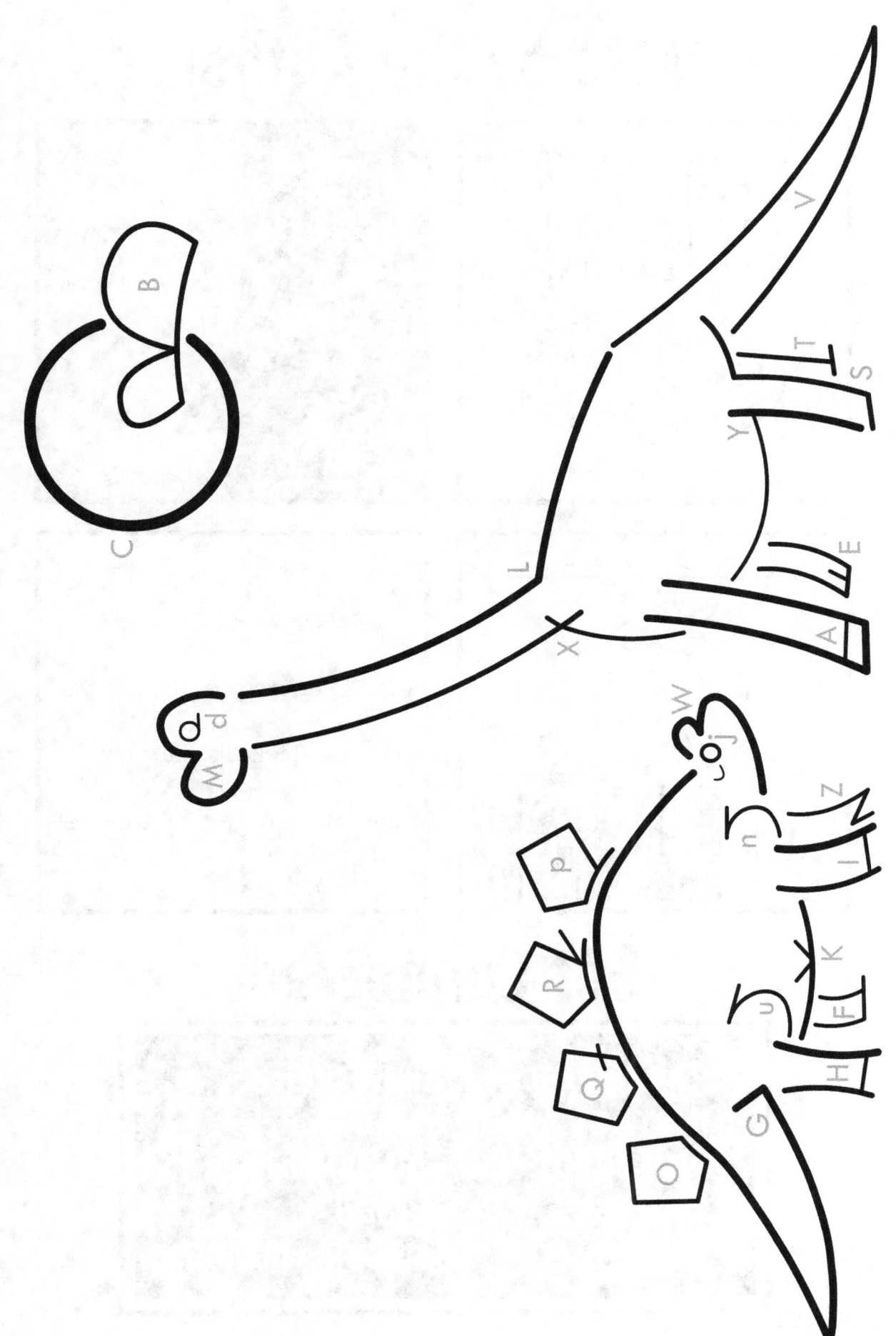

Also by the Author

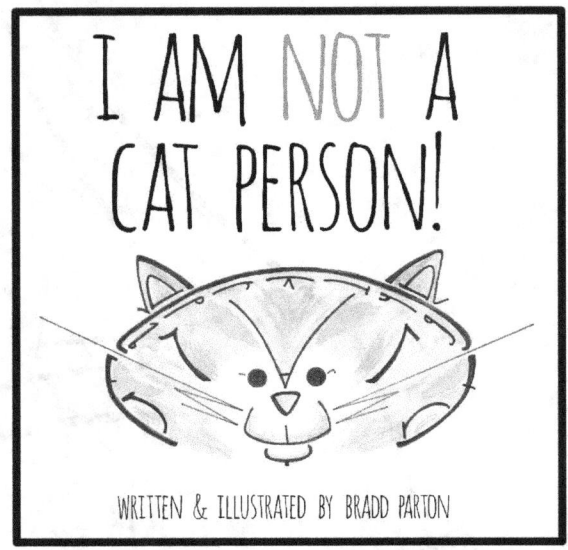
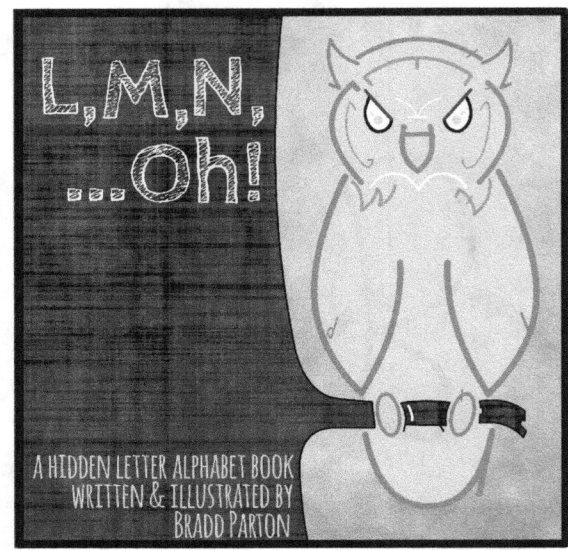

Visit Alpha-Sketch.com

for greeting cards, shirts,

prints, stickers, magnets,

custom art, games, & more!

Get Connected

FACEBOOK: /alphasketch
INSTAGRAM: /alpha.sketch
PINTEREST: /alphasketch
TWITTER: @bradd
SHOP: alpha-sketch.com